Remember Who You Are

Also by Esther Hautzig

The Endless Steppe

The Seven Good Years and Other Stories of I. L. Peretz
(translated and retold from Yiddish)

Remember Who You Are

STORIES ABOUT BEING JEWISH

by Esther Hautzig

CROWN PUBLISHERS, INC.

NEW YORK

Published by Crown Publishers, Inc., 201 East 50th Street,
New York, New York 10022

CROWN is a trademark of Crown Publishers, Inc.

Manufactured in the United States of America

Library of Congress Cataloging-in-Publication Data

Hautzig, Esther Rudomin.
Remember who you are : stories about being Jewish / Esther
Hautzig.
p.   cm.
1. Jews—Fiction.   I. Title.
PS3558.A77R4   1990
813'.54—dc20   89-27633
                                          CIP

ISBN 0-517-57502-7

Book design by June Marie Bennett

10 9 8 7 6 5 4 3 2 1

First Edition

Especially for Mama and Papa
Walter, Debbie and David
and others I love

Contents

Introduction

These stories are, in my mind, akin to sketches or quick charcoal drawings that leave much to the viewers' power of observation and elaboration.

Storytelling, without sets or costumes, came to mind when I wrote them. I loved short fables and tales, published without illustrations, best in my childhood. I drew the most elaborate pictures for them in my imagination. I still do, though my childhood seems long, long ago and far, far away.

It was spent in Vilna, an ancient and peaceful town in Eastern Europe, set along a winding, lovely river. I was born there in 1930, when Vilna was part of Poland. Its modern history began when a Lithuanian prince built a hunting castle on a gentle hill in 1323 and declared it the capital of the Grand Duchy of Lithuania. The castle dominated the city when I was a child; it does so still, though it's not nearly as tall as the city's modern buildings.

From a hunting castle, Vilna grew into an important seat of learning, not just for Lithuania, but later for Poland, Russia and the Jews of Europe. It has the oldest university in that region, in fact the oldest university in the Soviet Union at present.

The YIVO Institute was founded in Vilna; the famed Strashun Library, publishing houses of books in Hebrew and Yiddish, Jewish secular schools and *yeshivot,* the Vilna Theater Troupe, were anchored there. The spirit and beauty of the city had a way of bonding people to one another. It was the place of our common roots. The roots extend to the next generation and hopefully also to those that will follow. My daughter, a true-born New Yorker, has said for years that, "We're just different . . . We're from Vilna."

My son claims that I'm covered with some mysterious substance that attracts all manner of things only from Vilna. In occasional exasperation he wishes that "You guys [meaning me only] all came from Montana." But when I asked David, at age nine, whether he'd like new curtains in his room he told me, "Neh, I'll stick with the old ones." I said they were so plain and old fashioned—they were, and still are, off-white with tasseled tie-backs—and he replied, "That's okay, Ma, I like them. It's like having a little bit of Vilna in my room."

When I first met my husband, many years ago, he said that being from Vilna must be a state of mind, not just a fact. He was quite right. Perhaps that is why so many of

the stories here are about people from my place of birth
and spiritual home. Napoleon called it the Jerusalem of
Lithuania.

In 1939, when Hitler and Stalin signed a short-lived
peace pact, Vilna was handed back to Lithuania and became
its capital yet another time. Its name reverted to Vilnius;
that is its name until this very day. When the three Baltic
countries—Estonia, Latvia and Lithuania— "joined" the
Soviet Union in 1940 (from which they now want to secede),
my parents, grandparents and I were deported to Siberia,
as capitalists and enemies of the people.

Other members of our family escaped deportation. I wish
they had all been sent with us to the steppe. After the Nazis
occupied Vilna in the summer of 1941, most of them, along
with the vast majority of other Jews, were either immediately
killed in street "actions," or slaughtered in Ponar. The
remaining fifteen or sixteen thousand men, women and children were herded into the infamous Vilna ghetto or concentration camps. Except for two of my mother's cousins,
an aunt and the child of a cousin in Kovno, none survived
the Holocaust.

After six weeks in cattle cars we were deposited in Rubtsovsk, a tiny village in the Altai region of Siberia. Curiously,
I read in *The New York Times* and *Time* magazine that Raisa
Gorbachev was born and grew up also in Rubtsovsk. Since
we are close in age, we might have gone to the same schools,
known the same people. I can understand her no-nonsense
approach, quick thinking, sometimes impatient manners. A
typical Sibiriachka, with no time to waste on idle chatter
and silly concerns.

We spent nearly six years in Siberia. I went to school there, made friends, learned how to survive no matter what life brought. Mama worked at first in a gypsum mine, later in a bakery, at construction sites. Her education in Vilna's excellent gymnasium, and university, were not exactly useful training. Papa was drafted into the army and fought along with Russian soldiers. Grandfather died in a slave labor camp, in another area of Siberia, hauling lumber at age seventy-two. Grandmother was with us in Rubtsovsk all through the war and returned with Mama and me to Poland in 1946. We met Papa in the industrial city of Lodz after he was released from the army.

Since Vilna was still Vilnius, the capital of Lithuania, and part of the Soviet Union, my parents had made the decision to live in "free" Poland rather than in the USSR. I hated every minute of our first weeks there and never grew to like the city. It merely became tolerable with time. I often dreamt of returning to the desolate beauty of the steppe. Sheer insanity, of course, but at sixteen most people have their moments of madness.

After nine months in Lodz, where I went to a small Yiddish-speaking school, attended Zionist group meetings, made and lost friends, we moved on to Sweden to await our quota numbers for entry to America. Another thorn in my soul.

Suspended in time and place, I could not go to school, nor read local newspapers or magazines, nor even go to the movies. Most of them were either English or French, with Swedish subtitles, none of which I understood. I had no friends my own age, so I spent most of my time practicing the piano, tagging along when my parents visited their friends, reading such books in Russian as I could find in Stockholm and an occasional newspaper or magazine in Yiddish or Polish. I refused to read anything in German, though I was passably fluent in it.

I was thoroughly miserable and then totally unhinged after a personal tragedy struck me while we were still in Sweden. "Heniek," one of the sketches, tells the story.

One of the few things that saved my mind and for which I did not need to know the language was music. The kind piano teacher in Stockholm, to whom my parents sent me at great financial sacrifice, gave me some of her tickets to recitals. One of them was to be played by a young, Vienna-born, American pianist named Walter Hautzig, who was on his first concert tour of Europe in the spring of 1947. I liked his face on the program and looked forward to hearing him play. At the last minute I got ill and could not go, but for some reason saved both my ticket and program.

In May of 1947 my parents, who must have been driven crazy by my bleak mood and depression—though they staunchly denied for years that I was difficult—sent me off alone to New York. My mother's brother, Benjamin, who as a teenager in the 1920s had gone to live in America, arranged for a student visa for me, since Mama was convinced I might be thirty years old before I'd graduate from a secondary school. Our quota numbers for emigration to America seemed hopeless.

I left Sweden on the S.S. *Drottningholm* and on the boat met Walter Hautzig, in person, the same young man whose piano recital I had missed a month or so before. The sailing of the ship was delayed because of him, as he arrived in Göteborg harbor immediately after being decorated by the king of Norway. He received a medal in gratitude for concerts he'd played to benefit Nazi victims in Norway. I'd write much more about this wonderful man, and pianist, and husband, but he's at work on his very own book. I can no more steal his thunder in writing than I can while playing "Für Elise" on the piano.

I was seasick on the entire ten-day journey, so miserable that all I could do was lie on a deck chair and moan. Walter, and some other American and Scandinavian passengers on board ship, took me under their wings and were kind beyond measure.

When the boat docked in New York, Walter and my other guardian angels helped me get through immigration and customs in record time. However, Mama's brother, Benjamin, was told—I later learned—that the boat would come in at 2 P.M. It arrived at 10 A.M. and by eleven I sat under the letter R, for Rudomin, which is my maiden name, and waited. And waited and waited. To say that I was terrified would be too mild.

Uncle Ben, who not only sent me the visa, and affidavits for all of us to live permanently in America, and money and packages of all sorts of wonderful delicacies and clothes, but also kind and thoughtful letters, written in handwriting nearly identical to mine, did not arrive until 1:30 P.M. I'd never met him, but I remembered pictures of him from my childhood and had seen recent snapshots he'd sent to us from New York. Ten years after he left Vilna he married an American girl whose main passion was baseball, which made her truly exotic in my eyes, and had two children, Stanley, twelve, and Barbara, six. My American cousins. I had hoped that they would not find me odd, and that we would be able to communicate somehow. I missed my cousin Mussik, and my aunt Margola—of whom I write among the sketches—in the most intense, unrelenting manner. I still do. I was wild to have a real family again, with aunts, uncles, cousins.

Meeting Uncle Ben, and seeing how frantic he was when he realized he came late, is a moment in my life I shall always remember. I had been feeling sorry for myself, huddled on my suitcase on the nearly deserted dock; upon meeting him, I felt much sorrier for him. What's more, I adored him on first sight, and my love for him, and appreciation of his quiet, restrained manner in daily life, grew and grew. He could have been my mother's twin, they were so much alike in looks, in manner, in emotional makeup. Dark-haired, fair-skinned, with intense eyes but quiet ways.

Once in America I went to high school for one year in Brooklyn, where my uncle and his family lived, for two years to college in Manhattan, and then I married Walter just before my twentieth birthday. By then my parents were official residents of the United States, too. I entered publishing in 1951, on the lowest rung, but made my way and have been working in it ever since. We had two children, I wrote, and sixteen of my books were published; one of them about Siberia, *The Endless Steppe*, has been continuously in print for over twenty years and is still selling.

This book came about when Betty A. Prashker, a friend in publishing, and happily later the editor of these stories, suggested that I write a book on being Jewish, for that is what most defines me as a person. *On Being Jewish* was, in fact, the title I wrote on the first page, on the first morning, on beginning this manuscript.

I began to write it in the spring of 1988, at an artists' colony, Mishkenot Sha'ananim, in Jerusalem. Walter and I spent six weeks in Israel when he fulfilled a private pledge to himself to give freely of his knowledge and time to the Rubin Academy in Jerusalem. The academy, formerly called the Jerusalem Conservatory, saved him from the Nazis when he was a teenager in Vienna. Its director, Dr. Emil Hauser—who was also one of the founders of the Budapest String Quartet—took him out of Europe in 1938 and started him on the road to becoming the concert pianist and teacher he is today.

I went along on his coattails—and the full dress suit in which he performs does indeed have coattails—and was fortunate beyond belief to find the peace and time to write. We went back in the fall of that same year, when Walter played at the Musica de Camera Festival in Jaffa. During the second trip I was lucky to see Ada and Eddy, visit with Alik, Yakov and Chava, Manon and Roni, all wonderful people, all part of this book.

However, writing only on being Jewish in abstract terms, or from a historical or religious perspective, did not work well for me. I live it, breathe it, enjoy it, share it. But I could not write only of that. Instead I wrote about people whose lives had touched mine, whose fates changed my outlook on life forever, whose beliefs and practices inspire me and give me hope for humanity.

I wrote stories of those who are no longer here, and those who are still very much part of my life. Some are about people I think I know better than I know myself, others are about people I barely met, but feel I know in ways other than that which daily contact provides.

All, however, are told from the heart, with love.

Esther Hautzig

Remember Who You Are

Margola

My aunt Margola, who would have been over seventy years old this year, died before she was twenty-five. She perished during the Holocaust, in the Vilna ghetto; horrible, but not unusual. Millions of other Jews died in Europe in the 1940s. That one can say this almost matter-of-factly is horrifying in itself. She is but a nameless statistic to the historians of the Second World War. To me she will never be a statistic. She was my aunt, a vivacious young girl, giggly and conspiratorial, charming and clever.

When I was born she was only twelve years old. After seeing me for the first time, she told my mother that she had made absolutely no plans to become the aunt of a wrinkled red frog who wailed a lot. Immediately after I was brought home from the clinic where I was born, and as long as we were together, she brightened every day of my life.

1

Our times together, when I was growing up, are still the brick and mortar of my emotional makeup.

I saw my first performance of *Swan Lake* in her lap. Papa had ordered loge seats for Mama and me but I begged her to let me sit with Margola and all of her friends in the uppermost reaches of the balcony. No other performance of *Swan Lake* has given me equal pleasure no matter who danced it, for never again did I see it with Margola's arms holding me close.

Of all the photographs taken in my childhood those of Margola and me blowing bubbles on a large veranda in the country were the most precious. I'd gladly give up many photos of me in America for one likeness on paper of Margola and me that day in the summer. All of my childhood pictures with her were destroyed, but memories of them, as well as of her in life not in albums, help me recall her.

This tiny young woman, with black wavy hair and deeply set, but mischievous dark brown eyes, dressed in brightly colored cottons in the summer, and in winter in the sedate uniforms of the gymnasium from which she graduated with honors and of the university where she majored in chemistry. I had always dreamt of looking like Margola and wearing the same university cap, at the same rakish angle, so becoming to her dimpled face.

Margola had dozens of friends who regularly descended on our house, en masse, especially after my parents had had one of their fancy parties and mountains of delicacies were left over. Their noise and laughter, their intelligent faces and heated discussions, which I loved if not always comprehended, are a vital part of my memories of growing up, and are still with me in my middle age.

Her mother, Sonia, was also my mother's mother, but not the one who gave her birth. Grandmother Sonia was all a stepmother was not supposed to be. She adored, equally and unconditionally, her natural children, Margola and my uncle Liusik, and the children my grandfather had had with his first wife who died at twenty-three, in childbirth. There was nothing in the world she would not do for each of her children.

When Mama was planning to go from Vilna to the 1939 World's Fair in New York, she discussed with Grandmother all of the things she had to do before sailing for America. One day all three of us were sitting at our dining-room table; Mama and Grandmother were again going over the many details. First and foremost, and seemingly dreaded, passport photographs had to be taken. (Mama disliked being photographed as long as I could remember.) "Don't worry, my child, I'll run down to the photographer's now and have pictures taken for you." All three of us collapsed in laughter that time; recalling it now brings a different reaction.

Mama never did go to the World's Fair. Margola got ill with pneumonia and everyone was afraid that it would develop into tuberculosis. Instead of taking a boat to New York, Mama took her sister for a cure near Zakopane, which had the best skiing slopes in Poland as well as a number of sanatoriums for people with lung trouble, and brought her back to Vilna restored to good health.

Margola had my mother's special love; sometimes, it seemed, more so than I did. When Margola walked through the door, Mama's usually somber, and often severe face would dissolve in what can only be described as unadulterated *naches*, that special joy in another person, most often in one's child. If I was jealous, I was not aware of it then, or now. The smiles and glow Margola evoked in my mother reflected on me as well.

When the Second World War tore everyone's lives to shreds, we were deported to Siberia by the Soviet government as capitalists and enemies of the people. Grandmother Sonia, Margola, Liusik and countless other relatives were spared deportation to the steppe. They met a far more ignominious fate. Death. By shootings in the streets. By having to dig their own graves and then being shot into the gaping holes. By deportations to Dachau, Buchenwald, Auschwitz. The means of death were varied and many.

For a short while, I had heard, Margola, Liusik and Grandmother hid in an airless attic, with other members of the family. There Uncle Liusik silently studied and repeated algebraic equations and abstruse calculations in physics, which were his double majors at the university. He said that this alone preserved his sanity during the time he still had on earth. He perished in a concentration camp in 1942 or 1943.

But Margola might have lived. She chose to die when she was only twenty-three years old. Two cousins of my mother's, who survived the Vilna ghetto and the camps, told me how and why she chose what she had chosen.

The "actions" that took place in the Vilna ghetto nearly every day, marking people for camps or instant death, were scenes of unspeakable horror. Being sent "Right" meant going to a camp, which still held a promise of possible survival. "Left" meant Ponar, a peaceful meadow outside Vilna where, during those terrifying times, people dug their own graves, were shot, thrown in and covered with dirt.

My mother's cousins, and their mother, whose face they covered with red dye of some sort and whose hair they darkened with charcoal, were commanded to the "Right" during one such "action." Life still seemed to hold out some hope for them. My Grandmother Sonia, her hair white and her pale face prematurely old, was commanded to the "Left." Certain death awaited her.

Margola was sent to the "Right" with my mother's cousins. After a few minutes among the "spared" souls, she began to make her way to join the group standing on the "Left." None of the intense cajoling and whispered imploring by those around her, including the cousins', broke her resolve to walk to to the spot where her mother stood, awaiting death. She would not abandon her to face her last moments on earth without someone who loved her more than she loved herself.

When I heard this story, some years later, from my mother's cousins, my heart cracked, a crack that never healed. Rabbi Menachem Mendl of Kotzk said, hundreds of years ago, "There is nothing more whole than a broken Jewish heart." It is not true of mine.

For years I'd considered Margola a heroine. Yet when a cracked heart rules one's brain, doubts begin to seep through the cracks. Doubts that bring feelings of guilt, anger at the person responsible for these feelings, and at oneself, and anger at people who consider Margola's actions foolish rather than heroic.

"After all, what could she have done, what did she do to spare her mother's life, except lose her own?" This, with variations, has been said to me by people of different backgrounds, ages and religious beliefs.

The group on the "Right" with which she would have gone to camp was "lucky" to be interned in a working camp in Estonia. Many, many people there died. But some survived. Margola might have been one of the survivors, too. My mother's two cousins, and their mother, were. So were a number of their friends, an extended family forever after.

Margola might have come to America or Israel. She might have become a chemist, wife, mother. She would have been a cherished sister, aunt, colleague, friend.

When I became a mother and gave my firstborn my aunt's name, I thought of it as an expression of love for my daughter as well as a tribute to Margola. Years later it was not perceived as such. When my daughter was old enough to question her middle name, and later still when she was old enough to dwell on its implications, as she perceived them, she did not think of Margola as a heroine. To her she seemed an impulsive, improvident young woman. What good did her deed bring? Two deaths? Whom did she save? Her mother? Herself?

My daughter is loved and loving, she is deeply involved in family matters, current and past. But she cannot fathom why I consider Margola's lonely walk from the "Right" side to the "Left" side to join her mother in death a heroic act.

When I asked one of my mother's cousins whether it was uncommon for anyone from the "Right" to choose going over to the "Left" in an "action" her expression darkened. "Oh, very uncommon," she said. "How could it have been otherwise? Who would choose it?"

She remembered a gorgeous little three- or four-year-old girl in the group on the "Left," screaming frantically for her mother who was obviously somewhere among the people on the "Right." The Nazi guard, who seemed to have pity in his face, held the child aloft and begged the woman who was the child's mother to identify herself. Perhaps he wished to give the little girl some solace in her last hours on earth. Or maybe he wanted to have one more victim to shoot. Not one of the women on the "Right" came forward to claim the baby as her own. That, said my mother's cousin, is one of her worst memories of the war. It haunts her dreams. A screaming, hysterical child, in the arms of a Nazi who might have had pity, and a mother who wanted to save her own life instead of comforting her child in that child's last hours of life on earth.

An unspeakable act. Or was it? It happened between children and parents, brothers and sisters, cousins and friends. The urge to survive was—still is—stronger than the urge to be a savior. Perhaps *martyr* is the better word.

The question of what I might have done, might still have to do, has burdened my thoughts to an extreme degree. What *would* I have done? I loved my mother enough to do that, I think. That she loved me more, and would never even be plagued by such a question, is something I need not even consider. I *know* she would not have abandoned me on my last day on earth. Or might she have? What primal feelings are stronger? Self-preservation or the remote chance of preservation of those we love? Is love of others ever greater than love of one's own life?

In Margola's case it seems not to have been a consideration. She acted heroically, I think, in a world where heroism, morality and reason nearly vanished. And yet I wish to God she hadn't been so heroic.

Mussik

I'm an only child now; have always been one. But when I was growing up in Vilna we lived in a multiple dwelling house, along with my paternal grandparents, three uncles and two aunts and their spouses and children, and so I was never lonely.

The house was owned jointly by my mother and my father's family. It took up a corner of two streets in the main section of town, close to my father's family business, near the library, the theater to which the entire family went quite regularly, and not far from my school.

Each of the apartments faced a common garden. There were, however, two courtyards. One had a low stone building with a loading platform. At times machinery, sold by my father's firm, was stored there. The smaller courtyard had a little hill, either built over the years by my grandfather's

9

constant turning of the soil for his trees and flowers, or by nature itself. The hill was there for my cousins and me to slide down when snow came. Each of us had beautifully crafted wooden sleds and we made an awful ruckus all winter long.

I was almost never alone. All in all, until the war broke our family to smithereens, there were ten of us in that garden, helping Grandfather with his planting, laughing, arguing, plotting practical jokes.

Mussik, my father's oldest and favorite brother's son, was my special soul-mate. To this day, nearly fifty years after I last saw him, he is still the soul-mate of my dreams and memories. Mussik was born almost precisely nine months before I came into the world, so he was the older brother I'd always wanted.

He was soft-spoken, gentle, delicate, in a family of rather assertive, energetic children. Certainly he was quite unlike his very athletic, no-nonsense, strong-willed sister, Sanna, and my other cousins.

Until we were sent to school, we were almost always together. Each of the families had their own governess for the children, but Mussik and Sanna's Moscow-born, devoutly Russian Orthodox governess liked my wonderful, resolutely Jewish Miss Rachel, so we got together nearly every day. Miss Marina and Miss Rachel planned wonderful excursions for us. We went to Miss Marina's church on occasion and Mussik and I inhaled the incense with enormous enthusiasm. The burning candles, long-robed priests, stained-glass windows and onion cupolas filled us with delight. At times we worried what our grandfather, a leading member of our synagogue, would say if he knew of our pleasure. Mussik decided to take it up with him while we were planting flowers one spring day.

"Don't worry so much, Mussik! Enjoying other people's religion and church won't convert you." Grandfather smiled at Mussik and me. We both heaved sighs of relief at Grandfather's words.

When all the cousins played together and arguments or fights broke out, Mussik mediated, settled disagreements, made us forgive each other, if we could, or at least leave each other alone so the rest of us could play. He was not the oldest child among the cousins, but in his quiet way he had authority on his side. We listened to him because he seldom raised his voice and we followed his lead because he had our trust.

After we began our formal education, Mussik in a Polish-speaking school and I in a Jewish folk-school, where every subject was taught in Yiddish (which I barely knew but quickly learned), we still managed to be together many hours every week.

When he was six, his father became gravely ill with cancer and was taken by Mussik's blond, quiet-mannered mother to Vienna for treatment. Not once; many times. It was a terrible time for the family, but at least its terrors were not hidden from the children. We knew that our uncle, Mussik's father, whom everyone in the family adored, was very sick with a terrible illness, and we were all asked to pray for his recovery. For me this awful year in our lives was mitigated, slightly, by having Mussik, and sometimes Sanna, spend longer periods of time with us in our apartment in the family enclave.

Sanna, over four years older than Mussik, considered us

beneath her station in life and pretty much ignored our play. Or perhaps she was more aware of the tragedy that had struck her family and could not be bothered by our silly games.

Mussik's father died despite all treatments. All the children in the family were taken to the funeral and to the burial in the family plot near Antokol, on the outskirts of Vilna. It was early spring, but still very cold and snow bedecked outside of town. I remember that we were all covered with heavy fur throws in the horse-drawn carriages taking us to the cemetery. Mussik, Sanna, their mother and, I think, our grandparents were being driven together. I was with my father's youngest sister and some other members of the family; neither of my parents was in the same carriage as I. But exactly who was with me on that solemn day I cannot remember.

What I do remember, vividly, is Mussik's posture in the carriage directly in front of ours. His head was turned back to look at us, at Vilna on the receding horizon, not ahead to the cemetery where his adored father would be buried. His face was not covered with tears, but the look in his eyes, just beneath the visor of his cap, his downcast shoulders, lowered head, are imbedded in my memory. To lose one's parent, I realized then, was the most awful, terrible, unthinkable tragedy to befall a child.

After their father died, Sanna and Mussik, especially Mussik, spent more time with us than ever. Their governess, Miss Marina, no longer took care of them. Their mother had to put many hours in the family business. Such were the arrangements if Mussik's mother was to continue receiving her full share of our family's business profits. Children in my family were not shooed out of rooms when adults talked. We seldom had to wonder what was going on.

After school Mussik and I went to the library together, we visited relatives on my mother's side of the family whose homes were scattered throughout Vilna. He adored them and they loved him dearly, too. His own mother's family lived far away. He hardly knew them, but dutifully wrote letters and made presents for their special days.

When I had to pay a call—quite different from an official family visit—on my eighty-five-year-old great-grandmother Reise, on my mother's side, I always begged him to come with me. This venerable, rich old lady's ways puzzled me and often scared me. She lived in a large and airy apartment, in which one room was reserved for chickens that laid eggs fresher than those she could buy in the marketplace. It was said that she also had her chickens prepared for supper by her own *shochet,* the ritual butcher, whose ways she trusted more than those of the meat market's owners.

She seldom gave nice treats: sweet cakes, nuts and cookies that were the standard, everyday fare while visiting relatives on unofficial calls. On official visits tables nearly collapsed under the weight of endless platters of meats and vegetables, kugels, salads, fruit and cakes. All great-grandmother Reise ever offered us were sour balls. Those "treats" made me doubt that she and the rest of my mother's family were truly related to one another or that she could possibly have any affection for Mussik and me, her oldest great-grandchild.

But Mussik would make it all well on the way home from

her house. First he'd say, "Oh, Bobbe Reise is such an old lady she doesn't even remember to put cake and cookies on the table." Then he'd produce some coins from his pocket (I never had any money as my parents did not believe in allowances), and buy us a Droste or Suchard candy bar to share on the way home. When he bought us ice-cream cones, instead of chocolates in the summer, Mussik watched the ice-cream vendor with eagle-sharp eyes. If he thought that I got a spoonful less than he did, he'd point it out politely to the ice-cream man or he'd insist I take extra licks from his cone. Food has a way of keeping memories sharp.

Just before the war broke out in 1939, Mussik, Sanna and I found a frightened small white kitten, with a black mark on her chest, hiding near the gate to our courtyard. I promptly scooped her up into my arms, named her Moorka, which means Blackie in Russian (just to be thought funny) and claimed possession.

An argument between Sanna and me immediately began. She said she saw the kitten first. I said I did. Mussik said nothing. He took no sides. I cried. Sanna yelled. Mussik shifted his slight weight from side to side. Finally he announced that I should take Moorka to my home and we would see tomorrow about its permanent place to live. Always the conciliatory voice.

Once I got Moorka home and my animal-doting father helped me fix a sleeping basket for her by the wall tile stove, and a little "bathroom" box in the small vestibule near the kitchen, nothing on earth would make me part with her. No angry words with Sanna or reasoning and cajoling on Mussik's part would work. It didn't need to. Mussik worked it out with Sanna. He and I took care of Moorka, fed her and cleaned out her newspaper-lined "bathroom" in my house, and Sanna had no duties, as well as unlimited visiting privileges and the right to take her next door to their apartment on the days I had music lessons or gymnastics after school. Not entirely equitable, perhaps, from Sanna's point of view, but Mussik's decision was law, even for his imperious sister.

Early in September of 1939 war came to Vilna. Air raids began. Bombs fell on the city. One day we left the door open and Moorka, frightened by the noise, ran out and never returned. Perhaps another child found her and took her in. Possibly she was killed. We all cried—Sanna, Mussik and I. By then it hardly mattered who had found or owned her. We just wanted her back or at least to know that she was safe somewhere else.

The noise of the exploding bombs, and the sirens, was as threatening as if the world was about to end, even if no bomb fell on our house. To make everything absolutely, totally unbearable, my father was drafted into the army and sent off to fight the German armies in western Poland. Mussik's father was dead and both our mothers had trained as first-aid nurses. When the sirens went off, both of them were to report to their stations and we were to report to our grandparents and go to our small, self-made shelter in the cellar.

One day Mussik and I decided to follow instructions we had received from some demented bombing expert in our schools. We were told to lie down under the window, as close to the wall as possible or by the side walls of a room, always away from a direct path from windows and/or doors. Reflecting on these directives now, I think the man was bent on murdering all of us. At any rate, that day Mussik and I were alone in his house when the sirens went off. Not having enough time to abide by the rule to go to our grandparents, Mussik decided that we should crawl under the beds in his room, as they were set on either side of a window, overlooking a large flower bed we had planted with Grandfather that spring. We lay quite still.

The air raid had passed, but we stayed under the beds. It was dark and quiet; both of us fell fast asleep. An eternity later, or so it seemed to us, our frantic mothers, an angry Sanna, worried grandparents, aunts and uncles finally found us and gave us a calling down I still remember with a shudder. Almost more than I remember the air raid itself, for I remember how Mussik protected me from punishment.

He took full blame. "She only did what I told her to do," he said over and over in his quiet voice, looking first in his mother's eyes, then in my mother's. I tried to assume responsibility for what I had done, but Mussik would hear none of it. Why I deserved such protectiveness and love I do not know to this day. It tortures me, because Mussik— good, kind, loving, fair Mussik—is dead and I am alive. I know he was a *truly* good person. I think I'm not really deserving of the fate God dealt me.

When the Nazis marched into Vilna in 1941, shortly after we were deported to Siberia, they immediately shot thousands of Jews at Ponar, a peaceful meadow surrounded by woods outside of the city. To me Ponar is not just a dreaded name in Holocaust history, such as Dachau, Babi

Yar, Buchenwald, Treblinka. It is not just one of six memorial spaces at Yad Vashem, the first Museum of the Holocaust high in the hills above Jerusalem, at which an eternal light burns. It is the place to which the Germans led Mussik's sister, Sanna, and their mother, along with many more members of my family and thousands of other Jews from Vilna, to dig their own graves and be shot directly into the holes.

Toward the end of his short life, Mussik was left alone to shift for himself in the abysmal, crowded streets of the Vilna ghetto. Perhaps the Germans thought that he could still work. Two cousins of my mother's who survived the war had seen him in the ghetto for some time after his mother and sister perished. He slept here or there, did this or that, scrounged for food but did not beg for it—one of the roaming children in the confines of the Vilna ghetto until they disappeared forever.

The fate that met Mussik, my cherished friend and cousin, brother, soul-mate, is not unusual. How many remember the countless other Mussiks of the world, except the few remaining members of their families, if such were lucky to survive? Who remembers the children who died and are only recalled in the words of a song, a dirge, that lists common names of Jewish children who no longer play under the trees and in the fields of Europe?

When I was very young, I was told by my grandmother that people who are remembered, and recalled by name, do not truly die. It is then that their souls and names become eternal. That is what keeps some survivors of the war sane. Never to forget does not only mean never to forget the war, the slaughter. To me it means never to forget the names of those who died, to pass them on to future generations, to keep their candles burning not just once a year, on their communal Yahrzeits, the memorial days of the Jewish calendar, or even in the heart-rending way they are recited and lit in the children's memorial at Yad Vashem, but at home, always.

At a memorial service for the victims of the Holocaust in Temple Ansche Chesed, my synagogue on the Upper West Side of Manhattan, a program was arranged at which each person gave a photograph of a loved one to one of our members and a writer on the fate of Jews in Europe. He, in turn, made slides to project onto a screen during the program. I did not trust him with the only picture of Mussik that I own, "borrowed" permanently from my old governess, Miss Rachel, who now lives in Jerusalem. She had four or five faded snapshots from Vilna; one of them taken with her and Mussik and me. Another of Grandfather holding me on his lap. I have none of the many photograph albums from my childhood. They were all lost to me by the war, a loss as keen as any I've endured during my life.

And so I took my precious photograph to a shop I fully trusted, where my son worked after school for many years. The shop, incredibly, "lost" it, too, for a week or ten days; misplaced behind some envelopes in one of their cabinets. Someone put it there for extra safekeeping. It felt like a mortal blow, the only reminder of Mussik's face I have outside my heart.

I did not think that I could speak at the program. But finally I decided to describe Mussik, with a blank screen next to me, on which his photograph was to have been shown. I described the sun hat that he wore in the picture, his half-crooked smile, so much like mine, his thoughtful eyes and delicate features.

And I described his person—his gentle ways, devotion to peaceful coexistence with everyone around him, all his many saving graces, none of which had saved him from the Nazis' onslaught. I'd been told by many friends, and some strangers who were present at the program, that they remember Mussik without a photograph as well as those people whose likenesses were on the screen.

I write of Mussik, a little boy of no lasting "accomplishments," one who did not leave behind a diary or a song hidden in archives of the Vilna ghetto, who performed no special, heroic acts, that he, too, may be remembered just because he lived for some twelve or thirteen years—no one even knows that—and was killed in an unknown manner.

He might have become a social worker able to mediate and help families keep their peace, or a lawyer settling serious disputes, or a doctor who could find a cure for cancer, or a veterinarian who'd know just what ailed a little cat. He might have become any one of many valued members of society, but he is dead now for almost fifty years. No one knows how he died or when, nor even where he is buried.

Uncle Dodzia

Uncle Dodzia, my father's young brother, escaped death in the ghetto and in Ponar. He nearly escaped death altogether.

He was tall, blue-eyed, fair-skinned, blond, almost as handsome as my grandfather. A real Viking. He somehow obtained false papers, passed as an Aryan and made his way from the Vilna ghetto to small towns nearby. Finally he went to a town in central Poland where he thought no one would know him.

At times he lived as unobtrusively as a mole. He also took calculated risks. Despite his audacity, bravery, remarkable nerve, someone in an out-of-the-way place denounced him as Jewish to the local S.S.

He was immediately arrested and shot.

Uncle Dodzia was the oldest son of my beautiful grandfather by his second wife, Anna, and he was Anna's favorite child. The first wife, my father's birth mother, died of TB when he was nine. Papa wrote recently that her beautiful countenance followed him all of his life. Grandfather was left to take care of my father and three older children until he married Grandmother Anna.

The oldest was Berta, a tall, handsome woman who wore large hats and old-fashioned but beautiful clothes. She seemed almost as old as Grandmother Anna, though I did not know why when I was a child. She was married to a hapless inventor, whose schemes nearly bankrupted the family business at times. I loved him, nevertheless, and their two children, Reisunia and Salik. Reisunia was bookish and always gave good advice on what stories to read. Her eyes were of different colors, one was blue gray, the other dark hazel brown. That set her apart in the clan of cousins. Salik and I were born on the same date, two years apart. We celebrated our birthdays together, not always to our mutual joy.

Aunt Berta, her husband and children were shot in Ponar, according to those who survived the carnage.

After Berta, there were three boys in the first chapter of Grandfather's progeny: Uncle Liolia, Mussik's and Sanna's father, Uncle Abrasza and my father.

My grandfather Solomon was the handsomest man I have ever seen, not just in my childhood, in my whole life. By the time I was born his hair was white and he had a small, neatly trimmed beard. In his youth, I was told, he was golden-blond like Dodzia, as were my own father and years later my son. Grandfather had blue eyes and a sunny smile, but what I loved most were his comforting hands.

When I was ill, he came to my room and took out a red kerchief from his back pocket. He waved it around my head and sang a brief melody. Then he put both hands on my head and moved his lips in secret prayer. An immediate sense of well-being engulfed me. Grandfather was a *gabbe*, an elder, in his synagogue and a very observant Jew. He wasn't a faith healer who simply muttered magic words, but his personality was so magnetic, his large palms and fingers so loving, so healing, that to this day I believe that laying on of hands can cure all manner of ills.

His magical personality affected all who knew him. When Grandmother Anna, who was with us in Siberia, told me while we were walking on the steppe, that the four older children, Papa among them, were not his and hers, I was stunned. I asked her, as we walked to our patch of ground to weed potatoes, how she could be sure that she loved this stranger, this man who'd already had four children with another wife. She laughed then and laughed each time she repeated this story.

"You should have seen Grandfather when he was young! He was so handsome, so kind. He played the gramophone when I came to visit from Latvia. Sometimes we danced to the music!" When they first met she was in her mid-twenties, he about forty.

Now, when I'm not much younger than Grandmother Anna was when we spoke on the steppe, I'm no longer incredulous. Aging is a great equalizer.

Grandfather and Grandmother Anna had two other children after Uncle Dodzia, whose Hebrew name was David. Her second son was named Sioma, Shimon in Hebrew, and the youngest child was a charming daughter nicknamed

Sonitchka, Sara in Hebrew. I remember all three of them with clarity, not behind a scrim that often descends on recollections from childhood.

Uncle Dodzia was also a man to make young women swoon. He looked and acted like a glamorous movie star. When he entered a room he did not walk in; he swept in, hat tilted slightly to one side, or held elegantly in his hand. A fashionable raincoat was often draped on his shoulders. All of us, his nieces and nephews, governesses, housemaids, made way, greeting him like royalty. Grandmother Anna's adoration of this son was so consuming that in his very old age my father sometimes shakes his head, remembering their youth. "That Dodzinka, he got everything he ever wanted . . ."

Not quite.

Uncle Sioma, two years younger than Dodzia, was almost as good-looking, though his hair not so golden and his eyes not as blue as his brother's. He was a bona fide daredevil in Vilna, who rode around the city on a motorcycle, with a back seat and side car.

Sometimes, when he wasn't tootling around with one of his girlfriends, he'd take us along. We'd race around the city, Mussik and I, Sanna and Aunt Berta's daughter, scared out of our wits, holding our breath, exhilarated and elated at being grown-up enough to accompany Sioma.

After he'd had one scrape too many, Mama, who adored him but did not trust his judgment at the wheel, forbade him to take me for rides. I protested and wailed but Mama had made up her mind. The rest of my cousins were eventually forbidden these excursions as well.

In 1938 Uncle Sioma was allowed to take time off from

his duties in the family business, in which all the brothers worked, to visit Palestine. He came back just before the war broke out in 1939, married a gorgeous, exotic woman named Ava; they had a daughter just before the German invasion. All three were killed by the Nazis, Ava and the baby in Vilna, Sioma in a camp in western Poland.

Fair-haired Sonitchka had dark hazel eyes and a flashing smile. She married a successful young lawyer named Misha who was as dark-haired as she was blond. His skin was as swarthy as hers was translucent. At first he seemed like a foreigner in the midst of the family. But, like Dodzia and Sioma, he was the object of our intense admiration.

Misha rolled his own cigarettes and smoked them from a gold cigarette holder, held elegantly in his fingers. Theatrical, all three of my young uncles: Dodzia, Sioma and Misha. They were our own Three Musketeers—we adapted Dumas's novel to fit our own script. We watched them with awe and admiration, hoping that their glamour would some day rub off on us. That day never came.

Sonitchka and Misha had a son, whom I was permitted to swaddle when I came to visit. They lived in part of my grandparents' huge apartment, remodeled and furnished in the latest style, with blond furniture from Scandinavia and closets built into walls, both unusual for Vilna in those days. All three of them were killed; Sonitchka and her cheery, gurgling baby at Ponar immediately after the Nazis stormed in. Misha, we'd heard, was killed during a street "action," not in a camp.

Uncle Dodzia also married. His wife was gentle and quiet, with large dark eyes and very short black hair. We'd heard whispers among the housemaids and governesses that Musia was *old*. Older by two years than her handsome husband. She seemed to me more like my older aunts than Dodzia seemed like his older brothers. When Dodzia swept in, she followed him quietly. She was like Mussik's mother and mine, conservative, reserved, elegant.

Aunt Musia and Uncle Dodzia had a son, Grandmother Anna's darling, but a small and noisy "terror" in our midst. My father, too, recalls the storms this golden-haired, gorgeous child created in our garden. Mussik had to use his most persuasive manner to stop us from banning him from our games in summer and sled rides in winter. After his outbursts, our cousin would cry and hug us and plant sloppy kisses all over our faces. He'd promise "never to do it again" but he always did, and we always forgave him.

Aunt Musia and her son were killed during the first year of Nazi occupation of Vilna. We heard of it and of Uncle Dodzia's terrible fate when we returned to Lodz from Siberia.

I learned only a few years ago how Dodzia managed, for a time, to elude the Germans. We were returning from a funeral for one of my mother's best friends. In the car with us were Ida and Nechamia, old friends from Vilna who posed as Karaites and wandered from town to town with false papers during the war. We spoke of others who survived through illegal documents and I mentioned my uncle's sad end. Nechamia and Ida not only knew about Dodzia's death, they saw him twice along the escape trail. They offered to tell me all they knew of Dodzia as well as their own remarkable and harrowing story.

The Karaites believed in the Torah, the Five Books of Moses, but they did not follow much of Judaism's later teachings. Vilna, and its suburb named Troki, had the largest communities of Karaite followers in Europe; the vast majority of this sect lived in Turkey.

At the beginning of the war, Nazis treated Karaite followers as they did Jews and Gypsies, and other "undesirables." A short while later, however, an edict from Hitler was received in Vilna. Karaites were to be exempt from persecution.

Ida and Nechamia knew a lawyer who was nearly always drunk, anti-Semitic and greedy, but since he had long-standing dealings with the Karaite community, they decided to seek his help. This took place at the very beginning of the Nazi occupation in Vilna, when such negotiations were still possible for those with strong nerves and money. When they made contact with this lawyer, Ida and Nechamia pretended to be brother and sister, as they did until the war ended.

The lawyer drew up bogus, but official-looking, papers, stamped with seals containing Karaite symbols, and sold them to our friends. They immediately made their way from Vilna to a small town some fifty kilometers away. Fortunately they did not meet anyone they knew on the way. The officials in the prefecture of that small town were still local bureaucrats, not S.S. troops, and their palms were amply greased with gold pieces that Nechamia smuggled out of Vilna. The bureaucrats issued legal passports for this "brother and sister" with which they could travel throughout Poland and other German-occupied territory.

Before they left that small town, they met Uncle Dodzia, whom Nechamia knew in Vilna. While Nechamia continued the story of seeing my uncle, he felt he had to interject a memory that made him smile even as he was speaking of the tragedies in each of our families.

When he was young, he'd pass my grandparents' place on the way home from school. It was in a suburb of Vilna, right by the river. By May or June it would already be warm; he and his friends plunged into the river from small rafts and a dock by my grandparents' door. When they came out of the water, Grandmother Anna would ask them inside, set out freshly baked bread with sweet butter, and large pitchers of milk. She urged them to eat all they wanted, to have a good time.

"So, I knew Dodzia before we met in 'the fire.' "

During their occasional encounters in the small town, which to Nechamia was "fire," he and Dodzia talked briefly and surreptitiously. After a few weeks both Nechamia and Ida, and my uncle, decided to move on, though of course not together. They spent the rest of the war years on the run, several times facing death at the hand of informers. Luck, their Karaite documents and cool heads under inconceivable duress and danger saved Ida and Nechamia from a fate like my uncle's.

They ran into Dodzia next in Slonim, a larger town, farther from Vilna. In Slonim, Nechamia noticed that Dodzia had grown a bushy, bright blond mustache, which was to assure him an even more Aryan appearance. Many Jews seemed to think, Nechamia said, that having a mustache would make them look less Jewish.

In Slonim, Dodzia, in his Three Musketeers manner, held a job in the city prefecture, in an official capacity of some importance. Who would think of a Jew hiding in city hall, holding a title? Only the bravest, and smartest, would consider such action. Nechamia and Ida stayed in Slonim awhile, too. When they last saw my uncle, Dodzia said that it was getting dangerous to continue his pose. He planned to move to a small town near Warsaw, where he could hide until the war was over. Ida thought that by the time he'd made plans to move on, he was accompanied by a Gentile woman. Nechamia looked at her sharply and disagreed with her recollection.

That was the last time they'd seen Dodzia. The rest was hearsay, and rumors, then reports of people who'd heard from a reliable source that in the little town near Warsaw, my uncle Dodzia, with his blond hair and blond mustache, and totally Aryan appearance, was betrayed to the Gestapo and killed because he was Jewish.

Despite the fact that in 1946 Grandmother Anna was told that her children were killed by the Nazis, that Dodzia was shot at the instigation of an informer, she would not believe it. Until the end of her life, at eighty-eight in Israel, she held on to hope that at least one of her own children would miraculously appear, that people had made a terrible mistake when they said that Dodzia was betrayed and destroyed by a bullet.

Part of this tenacious belief must have been born during one of our walks in Lodz. One day after the war we passed a photographer's window and I, as always, stopped to examine all the pictures on display. Suddenly I noticed a photo of three men. The man in the middle uncannily resembled my Uncle Dodzia, but his raincoat was not draped over his shoulders. He wore it. His hat, however, was tilted in typical Dodzia style and angle. In the heat of the summer I stood frozen to the sidewalk, unable to move or speak. Grandmother followed my eyes and let out a piercing wail:

"My Dodzinka!"

We rushed through the door and asked hysterical questions of the young clerk behind the counter. "Who are the men in the picture in the window? No, not the men, just the man in the middle? He's wearing a raincoat!" The clerk and the photographer who came out from the back had no idea. It was some old picture they'd found in their boxes, they displayed it because it was a good photograph.

I passed by the shop countless times that summer. Sometimes I was convinced that it was not Dodzia. Other times I was sure it was my uncle. Mama and Papa went several times to the photographer's shop. Grandmother must have gone daily for months, imploring, questioning, seeking some answer. Maybe her son was alive somewhere in Poland? Why else would his picture hang in their window?

Though we weren't sure that the photo was Dodzia, we ordered a copy. Grandmother did not want anyone but her son in the picture; she had the photographer remove the other men's figures. Who knew, perhaps one of them betrayed her son? And then, perhaps, he was a friend who mourned his death?

Perhaps the picture provided hope to Grandmother Anna, perhaps she lived as long as she did because she never gave up thinking that her Dodzinka would find her in Tel Aviv or Holon, in Rishon LeZion or Jerusalem. He'd look for her all over Israel!

I have a copy of the photograph; showed it to Nechamia. He assured me it is Dodzia.

Without a mustache.

Heniek

My best friend after the Second World War, a young boy of seventeen, survived the dreaded Lodz ghetto in western Poland, and Theresienstadt as well. So did both his mother and his father. A true miracle had occurred. The whole family, all three of them, were reunited after the war and returned to live once more in their native Lodz.

Less than two years after the war ended, Heniek committed suicide, on the roof of an abandoned building in what so recently had been the Lodz ghetto, where he had eluded death for nearly a third of his short life.

He had dark, very curly hair, which he was constantly taming into submission with fistfuls of vaseline. He dressed immaculately, in well-pressed slacks and neat shirts and jacket. Heniek was careful and vain about his appearance; in Lodz, so soon after the war, that was not easy. Clothing

was at a premium—most of it donated by charitable organizations and individuals in the United States, and much
of it unappealing and inappropriate. Heniek, however, either
had good luck in finding clothes that fit him, or money to
buy them in one of the shops that were opening on the main
streets of Lodz.

We met in September 1946, in the tiny, informal I. L.
Peretz School. Our classes were conducted in an apartment.
All the students were survivors of the war, many sad and
silent, some rambunctious and eager to make up for lost
time. Heniek was thought to be the handsomest, brashest,
devil-may-care fellow. The girls adored him. The boys liked
him, too. He played the accordion and had a deep baritone
voice. He sang at the slightest hint that a song was welcome.
The girls practically swooned over his "performances," and
the boys laughed at his jokes and repeated them to each
other.

But he was *my* special friend. Everyone knew it.

Heniek and I also worked together after school. We
were assigned by our teachers to duties in a group home
for children who had been rescued by Gentiles and who
were being returned to the Jewish community—voluntarily
and under pressure as well. A large apartment was especially
set up to house these children and to make their lives and
transition periods as comfortable and painless as possible.

Many of the young boys and girls were awaiting transport
via Paris to Palestine. Others were going to be reclaimed
by relatives of their dead parents and taken to America or
Argentina, South Africa or Australia.

The children ranged in age from five or six to fourteen.

I was assigned to tutor a twelve- or thirteen-year-old boy who had reverted to totally infantile behavior by the time I met him. He could not or refused to read. He wished to be held like a baby, tucked in at night in bed, as if it were a crib, to hear an endless stream of lullabies and fairy tales.

This boy insisted on being spoon-fed and lifted up and down into chairs and his bed. Since he was nearly as tall as I, and a great deal stronger, I needed Heniek's help. The boy refused to be looked after by anyone except me after I'd appeared at the home three afternoons a week. He tolerated Heniek as long as both of us paid attention to him alone.

Heniek's gentleness and quiet firmness, too, when "our boy" became unruly, his endless patience with the other children at the home, who were scared and angry one day, jubilant and expectant another, showed another side of the brash and boisterous personality I knew in school.

Heniek and I, and some other of our schoolmates, also belonged to a Zionist youth organization and we met for discussions, arranged folk-dance evenings, planned for our futures. Would all of us wind up on the same kibbutz in Palestine? Would we even get into Palestine or be returned to Poland by the British or interned in Cyprus?

Would a pogrom break out in Lodz as it did in nearby Kielce, where over thirty Jews, survivors of concentration camps, were killed? Would anti-Semitism ever end? Would we escape it if we left Poland for the Promised Land, or for other places on the face of the earth? So much to look forward to, so many fears.

After months of being together constantly in school, in

the group home, during our Zionist organization meetings, Heniek and I tried to find time to be alone, to talk only to each other, not always in groups. Since there was no privacy where he and I lived, we walked endlessly during our free time, all over the streets and parks in Lodz. When the weather was nice we sat on benches, or, money permitting, had ice cream or small pastries, in a little shop not far from school.

It was during these talks that I found layers of anger underneath the outer cover of Heniek's complicated nature. He wanted to live life on *his* terms. Life *had* to be perfect. Hadn't we all had enough? Shouldn't our futures be absolutely harmonious, just the way we want them? I listened, sometimes murmured assent, sometimes disagreement. It did not seem to matter to him what my reactions were, as long as I listened. Since I cared about him deeply, it was the least I could do.

When we had dates, in the American sense of the word, and went to movies or the theater, he would become terribly agitated if a performance to which we'd planned to go was sold out. When I tried to calm him, say that it was unreasonable to become so angry about such a small, unimportant matter, he would explode in rage. He did not consider it unimportant, he'd shout. He'd had enough. To me it seemed unreasonable—then.

Life had its irritations for me, too, but I didn't let my anger show. We had survived, after all. Wasn't that all that mattered? I held my anger deep inside me. It wasn't until years and years later, when I was close to middle age, that I'd heard an interview with Bruno Bettelheim on the Dick

Cavett show. At last I understood Heniek, and myself, too. Cavett asked Bettelheim whether survivors of the war were better able to cope with everyday life's irritations and losses. After all, Cavett said, what were these compared to the hell of war?

Dr. Bettelheim replied that, in fact, survivors have far fewer resources for coping with life, less mental stamina and emotional reserves. How true, and how simple it sounded when heard in New York, and how helpful it would have been to hear such words in 1946 and 1947 in postwar Poland. Heniek's rages and my reactions to them might have been different, and my own, far less difficult problems easier to understand.

When my mother, grandmother and I got back to Lodz from Siberia, after the war, and were reunited with my father, I was afraid to leave our room to walk on the street, use a trolley car, go into a shop, function in a normal manner. I found that I hated "civilization." Siberia seemed safer. Life after the war was not supposed to be lived in the dark, one-room apartment Father found for us. It was not supposed to hold beds for all of us in one tiny space, nor to have a stove, a wash basin, chairs and small table all practically on top of our beds. And no sunlight.

"After the war" meant to me my sunny, spacious home in Vilna, with the curtains blowing in the wind, the colorful kilim rug in Father's study, the blue brocade walls in the dining room, the lilac bushes blooming in our garden, delicious foods of all kind, everything precisely as it was when I was seven or eight years old and considered my life absolutely perfect.

It was not to be, and so I wouldn't face it, but I could not bring myself to rage and carry on about my disappointment. I felt I would be letting everyone down. After the war there were no teams of trained social workers, or psychologists, to help us get over whatever traumas we had faced for years. We coped as best we could. Mother finally took me to a family doctor who suggested that she buy me a set of cheap dishes and let me break each plate, one after another. Of course, since we had no money for a set of dishes to eat from, let alone break, the idea fizzled. My inventive mother, however, collected stacks of newspapers from everyone she knew and made me tear them sheet by sheet into thin strips. This tactic must have helped to some degree.

A cousin of my mother's, who survived the Vilna ghetto, and a concentration camp in Estonia, along with her mother and sister, helped me even more. She came one day, commanded me in no uncertain terms to get dressed and stood over me with a determined, no-nonsense look in her eye. When I was finally deemed presentable, in a heavy navy-blue serge skirt and a white-and-blue georgette blouse, all neatly pressed, and looking almost new, she took my hand and practically dragged me out of the house. More than my mother had been able to accomplish.

Next thing I knew we were in a trolley car, bouncing up and down, swaying in a sea of people. It was late spring and already quite warm. I was covered with perspiration from the heat and my heavy skirt, as well as from the fear of noise, people, general commotion.

After returning home and realizing that I had not died

and gone to hell, I decided that perhaps I would survive "civilization" after all.

Heniek's wartime experiences could not have been compared to mine in any manner or form. Our five and a half years in Siberia were difficult, but it was not the hellhole the Lodz ghetto was, nor purgatory like a concentration camp. Where I lived on the steppe no one carried cyanide pills under tooth fillings. Heniek and his father did, to swallow in case they were led into the gas chamber. His emotional reserves were totally depleted during the war, though none of it showed in his demeanor in school, at the group home, at our Zionist organization meetings, and most of the time when we were alone, together. When Heniek was in control of his situation, everything was tolerable. When things got beyond his power, even small, unimportant things like scarcity of theater tickets, a short-circuit seemed to take place in his head.

Perhaps his parents did not see, or did not consider his attacks of rage important enough to act on. How could one *act* on such trival causes for agitation? I would try to kid him out of his "nonsense" or simply listen. What could one do when a person threw a tantrum over "nothing"?

He was, after all, one of the luckiest of the lucky. He survived the Lodz ghetto, and Theresienstadt, and his parents had survived as well. *He* had no cause for raging.

At the beginning of 1947 my parents had decided to try their wings in America, near my mother's brother, at Uncle Ben's insistence and at his expense. Heniek's parents also had family in America, but they seemed in no hurry to leave Lodz. His father was a highly trained professional, with a fine position. His mother had a good job as well. They, unlike my family, had finally found a more than tolerable place to live. A separate room for Heniek, a separate kitchen, proper bathroom. Important considerations when one had been cooped up for years in cells and crowded rooms.

Heniek's parents had a circle of friends among both Poles and Jews. There was no rush to emigrate from Poland. They'd see how life would continue for them in Lodz. To start again in a new country, with a new language and customs, seemed an unimaginable effort.

Heniek reported all of this to me rather quietly and evenly, too calmly in view of his rages at sold-out performances and skewered plans to meet on street corners. Even though I knew how much he wanted to leave Poland when we did, there were moments when I thought he did not really care.

Five months after Heniek and I met in school, my parents and I went to Sweden to await our quota numbers for entry to America. He stayed in Lodz, hoping that his parents would decide to emigrate later, or permit him, at eighteen, to go to Palestine. Someday we'd meet there.

He wrote me many letters to Sweden, nearly every day. Those letters were, in turn, hopeful and funny, forlorn and sad. Sometimes even cynical. But there never was a hint of anything more than disappointment at still being in Poland, occasional anguish at missing friends who'd moved away. Nothing like the tantrums he had had when we could not see an operetta, or buy a magazine he particularly wished to read. No threats of suicide—such thoughts never even entered my mind, nor that they might enter his. He never wrote that he had gotten a pistol.

The last letter I received in Stockholm from Heniek arrived in the same mail as the Jewish community newspaper to which we had subscribed to keep in touch with what was happening in Lodz. I read his letter first, of course, two or three times as was my habit, and then leafed idly through the newspaper. On the back page I found a small item about a suicide. On the rooftop of an abandoned building in the ruins of the former Lodz ghetto, Heniek C. had killed himself. A gunshot wound to his left ear inflicted instant death. The reporter said so.

That shot has reverberated in both my ears ever since that bleak, hope-killing day in Sweden.

Later I learned that my friends from the Zionist youth group sent me a telegram, informing me of the tragedy. My parents hid the news from me. This was so unlike the honesty and forthrightness I was accustomed to that I have never come to terms with it. Did they think I'd never find out? That I'd assume Heniek no longer cared and ceased writing? Would they really be able to protect me by their action?

I also learned, later, that Heniek's parents had made a final decision to remain in Poland and that they would use every means at their disposal to keep Heniek with them in Lodz. They did, but only in the cemetery, and not in consecrated ground at that. Suicides, in those days, were not even granted such repose.

Heniek's parents were not to blame. War was to blame, even after it was over.

Mira, Grisha and Their Daughter

This story is true. Only some names and identifying details are changed, for reasons that will become obvious to those who read it.

The daughter of my parents' friends from Vilna was saved during World War II by a Gentile woman from a nearby village. She was the girl's nanny before the war began. After the war, the girl's parents, both of whom escaped the Nazi slaughter by becoming partisans and fighting the enemy in woods and hamlets near Vilna, searched for her near and far. All their efforts met with failure.

The child and her caretaker, or savior, seemed to have vanished, even possibly to have been captured by the Nazis and killed. No one knew where they had gone, or no one would tell the couple, Mira and Grisha. When the search became completely futile, the couple moved on to Poland from Vilna.

Two sons were born to them in Poland, in 1946 and 1947. After a year or two in Warsaw, where Grisha built up a little business producing buttons and where the family lived reasonably well, they moved to Palestine. The land of milk and honey was far from sweet when they first arrived. The war between the newly founded State of Israel and all its Arab neighbors threatened their very lives and existence, but Mira and Grisha and the children were content to have come home, at last.

They were honest, simple people. They hadn't much education, nor finesse, nor any social graces. Their home could have been termed sloppy, their manner boisterous. Their hearts, however, were made of pure platinum.

Some years after the Holocaust in Europe ended, Mira and Grisha received a call in their little home in a suburb of Tel Aviv. A member of the Vilna survivors society in Tel Aviv wondered whether they would be able to come in for some blood tests within a day or two? They agreed, of course, not knowing precisely why such a test was needed so many years after the war but not daring to refuse or even question the request.

From past hearsay Mira and Grisha knew that, miraculously, survivors surfaced from time to time, as from a stormy sea. Blood tests were the only link that identified members of the family. Yet they dared not get their hopes up. Vanquished hopes were harder to live with than no hope at all—a statement I have often questioned, but more often agreed with. After all, weren't Mira and Grisha sure that their daughter vanished, without a trace? Hadn't they looked everywhere, followed every wild lead and met with bitter disappointments? Their most valiant efforts came to naught and here it was, almost a decade after they first started their search.

Of course they went for all the blood tests that were required and returned home to await the news of what the tubes of red fluid taken from their veins would show. In a few days, or maybe after a week, a call came to inform Mira and Grisha that their daughter, vanished long ago in Vilna, was living in Israel and searching for her family. The blood test proved it beyond question.

Grisha and Mira, hysterical and near shock, asked almost in unison whether the girl had a large birthmark on her right thigh. She did.

A meeting was arranged. The parents, their daughter and two sons, the girl's brothers, were united. All was to be perfection, utter harmony, a miracle on earth. The opposite took place.

The daughter who was saved disliked her birth parents on sight. She did not care for their loud way of speaking, their common, almost crude, manners; their unkempt home, tasteless food, the dowdy clothes they wore and bought for her, and even the fact that they did not strictly observe the religious rituals of the Jewish faith.

Her uncomplicated brothers fared no better in her eyes. Noisy, supercharged, often dirty. She could hardly bear them; called them uncouth, behind their backs and to their faces. The boys, seven and nearly nine years old, were humiliated and deeply hurt. It seems, though, that they bore their pain in silence.

Mira and Grisha learned that the Gentile woman who'd saved their daughter had turned the child over to a very genteel, highly educated Christian couple before the war ended. They had no children of their own and happily adopted the girl. Possibly this couple helped the nanny when she fell gravely ill, gave her money, food and medicine before she passed away. The woman told the truth about the girl's Jewish background, but assured the adoptive couple that her natural parents perished in the Vilna ghetto.

The girl turned out to be quick, clever, an excellent student. Beautiful, blond like her adoptive mother. Smart like her adoptive father, who, in time, became a judge and made his ten- or eleven-year-old daughter proud to be his child.

She went to church, took communion, practiced her mother's Catholic faith despite the Communist government in the easternmost area of Poland where they lived. She played the piano, brought excellent reports from school. A perfect daughter for the judge and his cultivated, quiet, elegant wife.

As the girl got older she grew combative, argumentative, rebellious. She tested her wings with great ferocity and anger. A normal teenager. One day she got into a fierce argument with her mother and said unspeakable things. Her mother retaliated by telling the girl that she should be grateful she was alive, that she was, in fact, a damned Jewess from the Vilna ghetto. Without the Gentile nanny who had saved her, the girl would be ashes in some concentration camp oven. Without them, the mother hissed, she would have led the hard life of a poor woman's child. She should be grateful for all she'd gotten from her parents! Didn't she get a lot? A fine home, good clothes, books, even a piano. On and on the mother ranted.

The girl did not have hysterics. She merely left the room

43

and her fuming mother, took some money from her father's desk, a change of clothes, and ran away from her "fine" home. That same day she was able to travel to the next town where she thought she would find a Jewish family or two. That she easily and miraculously accomplished. They, in turn, directed her to other Jewish sources, who made secret arrangements and paid her way for an ostensible visit to Paris. From France she was able to go to Israel through the help of an international Jewish youth group, and made her way to a kibbutz not far from Holon.

All done deliberately, efficiently, without histrionics. The knowledge that she came from a family who perished in the Vilna ghetto in the early 1940s prompted her to ask people in the kibbutz, nearly a decade and a half later, whether there were survivors from Vilna who might have known them. She did not know her true last name, but one lead brought another and the final one led to the blood test that was administered anonymously to every survivor who was known to have given a baby girl for safety to a Gentile person.

A small but vital detail helped to confirm that the girl's family was indeed from Vilna and that she had spent time in the ghetto with them. She recalled a song that she could have only heard in its confines. It was composed at the beginning of the war and sung to lull little ones to sleep. "Quiet, quiet, let's be silent, graves are growing here . . ." Chilling words, haunting melody, not easily forgotten, not even by a very young child.

Happiness should have reigned for Mira and Grisha, their newly found daughter and their carefree sons. But blood, alas, is not always thicker than water and it does not always bind people as they think it should.

After some fifteen years apart, the parents and their daughter had nothing in common save their blood and genes. They fought ceaselessly, over everything, including religion. Their daughter, reared a Catholic, seemed particularly appalled by their lack of attendance in synagogue, nonobservance of dietary laws of Kashruth, negligence in giving a proper religious education to the boys. Mira, Grisha and their three children went to synagogue. Mira made their home strictly kosher, arranged for religious instruction for her sons. It did not seem to work, did not bind them at all.

The daughter decided to "return" to her Catholic faith. The frantic parents accompanied her to church services in Jerusalem, desperately trying not to lose her. After all, they were not truly religious—a Catholic daughter was still their child and they loved her unconditionally. But whatever they did to build a bridge between them came to naught, undermined and washed away by floods of tears and recriminations.

The daughter came of legal age and moved away. Probably served in the Israeli army, as all adult Israelis must. To alleviate the constant agony, Mira, Grisha and their two sons left Israel and settled in New Jersey. Their daughter remained in Israel, refusing contact with her parents and her brothers.

My family and I never ask about her welfare. It only brings pain to the faces of her family in America. For years and years now it seems as if the daughter has ceased to exist or was never found at all. Grisha died. At his funeral, and during the seven days of mourning, *shivah*, no one I know presumed to ask for his daughter or even to mention her name. Mira is over eighty, the two sons are very successful businessmen with children of their own, leading fulfilling, charitable lives.

It is rumored that the daughter lives alone, possibly in Jerusalem, avoiding all contact with anyone who has connections to her childhood years in Vilna—a survivor of the Second World War.

Ada and Eddy

I've been thinking of Ada for over forty years, but I've met her only twice in all that time. Once, very briefly, in 1978 during our son's bar mitzvah trip to Israel, the second time for a long visit when we were there in 1988. I did not meet her husband, Eddy, in 1978. With Eddy at her side, in 1988, Ada was like a person in full daylight. Without him, when we met ten years before, she had seemed half hidden by shadows. Or perhaps I had just imagined it.

I knew of Ada all these years because she was one of the few members of my family who survived the war. She was saved in Kovno, by her Gentile nanny. She was born in 1938 and lived in Lithuania until she emigrated to Israel with Eddy in the early 1970s.

There was very little contact, and no exchange of visits, among the Kovno and Vilna lines in our family. Between the two world wars Vilna became part of Poland; Lithuania did not recognize the sovereignty of Poland over my hometown. It was like war, but without guns or shelling, and no visits were possible between the two countries.

Ada's grandmother and mine were sisters. Hers, in Kovno, was her father's mother, mine was my mother's birth mother, who died when Mama was three and Uncle Benjamin was born. I knew nothing about my mother's birth mother, though I was given her name when I was born. My mother worshiped her second mother—Margola's and Liusik's mother as well—and I loved my grandmother so intensely and completely that it would have been impossible to imagine any other woman as Mama's mother.

I had heard of Ada's grandmother Fania as Mama's aunt, and of Ada's father, Liova, as Mama's cousin. The exact bloodlines escaped my notice until 1940, when Vilna became Lithuanian once more, and I met Fania and some of her family for the first time. Fania, staying in our house, told me, without consulting my mother, that my beloved grandmother, Mama's adored mother, was not her *real* mother, that she was her stepmother.

This news provoked a cosmic storm that began when I cried, and yelled and stomped my feet, and wildly protested that the only *real mother* is the one who loves and takes care of her children, and grandchildren. It ended, I was told on good authority many years later, with a slap to Fania's cheek by the hand of my reserved, controlled, ladylike mother. The slight to my grandmother must have upset Mama to the depths of her being. She held me and kissed me and told me she was proud of my words. Where did I learn

48

them, she wanted to know. I could not explain. They came from the same source that made her slap her aunt Fania.

There were three aunts and one uncle on my mother's birth mother's side of the family. Their exact relationship to Mama and Grandmother never came up—until Fania's shattering news. They all acted like one big family, without boundaries or distinctions, and all of them, except Fania, lived in Vilna, so I saw them frequently in our home and theirs.

Fania was stern, dark-eyed, with an arched nose, like my mothers's, beautiful, coal-black hair, even in middle age, and a haughty manner. She received her graduate degrees in Berlin, where she met her husband, Cemach. Later Cemach became head of the most famous Hebrew gymnasium in Eastern Europe, in Kovno, Lithuania. It was the only high school in that whole area in which all subjects were taught in Hebrew and from which the diploma permitted entry to state universities. No small accomplishment for that time and place.

Fania's appearance and manner were unlike that of her sisters Nadia and Lisa, who lived in Vilna, nor like that of her brother Reuven, who lived just up the street from our house. Not one of them was dark-haired, dark-eyed or haughty.

Aunt Nadia studied in St. Petersburg, where she became involved with the revolutionary movement in 1905 and where a Russian officer fell in love with her. When she spurned him, he threw a bottle of lye in her face and nearly blinded her. When I knew Nadia, she was beautiful despite her scarred features and squinting, light gray eyes. Her hair was golden brown, pulled back in a bun that always fell apart and framed her delicate face. She and my mother's second mother, the one Fania called a stepmother, acted like loving sisters, one of the reasons, perhaps, that I never sorted out the relationships in Mama's family.

Some years later, the Russian revolutionary cause of 1905 behind her, Nadia married another extraordinary educator in my native part of the world. Leib, her husband, established the Reál Gynnasium in Vilna, in which all subjects were taught in Yiddish and which was recognized by the Polish educational and governmental authorities as equal to Polish gymnasiums and whose diploma was sufficient for admission to the state-run universities in my city. My mother graduated with the first class of that gymnasium, a landmark in the history of educating young people in Yiddish. Leib Turbowicz's Reál Gymnasium is known wherever Jewish culture and history are studied. Pictures of its founder and first graduating class, as well as pictures of Fania's husband, Cemach Feldstein, and his gymnasium, are in the archives, and sometimes on display at the YIVO Institute in New York.

The third sister, Lisa, also received a higher education, I think, but she chose to marry a gentle shopkeeper who dealt in notions and helped run their business. The family's embroidery yarns, lace, buttons, hooks, needles, hoops, canvas, thimbles, all the things I loved to buy and then work with, were purchased in Aunt Lisa and her husband's shop. Each expedition, for it was more that a mere shopping trip, was a treat.

The only surviving brother (an older brother died in

early youth), Reuven, was a very rich merchant. I remember that he had a fine long beard, wore a skullcap and black coat and was a short and jolly man. His wife was also small and of a cheerful disposition. They had several noisy children and grandchildren who filled their dining room with a racket seldom heard in other homes in our family.

Years later, after my son's first Hebrew teacher turned to Hassidism, and when I met and grew to admire wonderful members of the Lubavitch Hassidic community in Brooklyn and in the Old City in Jerusalem, I questioned my father about my somewhat surprising predilection for Hassidism. How could it have taken such a strong hold? I was educated in a totally secular school. Many members of our family followed the Haskallah, the movement that espoused the age of enlightenment; some were even Bundists, who were cultural, not religious, Jews. How could the life-style and tenets of the Hassidic community have such a hold over my feelings? My father immediately attributed this to Uncle Reuven's genes. He was, Papa said, a Hassid through and through. As far as my father was concerned that sealed my fate, though I only remembered Uncle Reuven's "different" clothing, not his religious practices and beliefs.

When I shared this twist in our common family history with Ada, she did not say how she felt about Hassidism, but she laughed uproariously. Her face reminds me a little of her grandmother Fania: both have dark, intense eyes. Ada's however, glisten with humor and kindness.

Ada's father, Liova—Fania and Cemach's oldest son— received a medical degree in Liege, Belgium, and at a very young age became one of Kovno's most distinguished sur-

51

geons. Their second child, a daughter also named Esther, for Fania's sister and my mother's birth mother, studied civil engineering in London. Toussia (which was her nickname) and her young husband went to Sumatra in the 1930s to build roads on that Polynesian island.

The youngest son, Shurik, was brought by his father to America, to study agriculture in Pennsylvania, in preparation for life in the Holy Land. He remained in his alma mater as a teacher, then dean of students, and at last president of the college. His father returned to Kovno in 1939.

All of Ada's family, those remaining in Kovno and those who went to Vilna just before the German invasion, were killed by the Nazis. Ada lived in the Kovno ghetto until its end was certain and her parents saw no way out. Her nurse smuggled Ada out of the ghetto at the risk of death—for both of them.

Ada told us the entire story in a restaurant overlooking Jaffa harbor, from which Jonah sailed to Tarshish thousands of years ago. I had heard parts of it before, but not directly from Ada. The dinner was elegant and the French food perfect. The atmosphere and the dishes served us did not mesh well with the tale she was telling, but that is the way of the world now. The old, once shabby Jaffa harbor has been transformed into a magnificent art center, with concert halls, galleries, shops, restaurants. Walter played there during a nearly week-long music festival before we saw Ada and Eddy.

Ada's nurse told her that there were Jews who dug secret caves to save their lives inside the ghetto. They were hounded out of hiding by fires set by Nazis, and shot on the spot by the S.S. or their Lithuanian accomplices. The rest of the ghetto was destroyed by mass executions and deportations to concentration camps.

Ada had heard from her nurse that the Lithuanian partisans tried to enlist her father to their ranks. His medical and surgical skills would have been invaluable to them. Ada's mother refused to leave her own mother in the ghetto and she, in turn, was unwilling to leave her own very old mother. All three—Ada's mother, grandmother and great-grandmother—perished, along with husbands, brothers, sisters, children.

I'd heard before that Ada's nurse not only saved her physically; she passed on to her what she knew of the heritage from which she came. As soon as the war was over, her nurse told Ada that she was Jewish. She told her all she knew of her family, how they lived and how they died. Not only she but her much older sister, who helped raise Ada's father, were part of the household.

Soon after the war ended, a distant cousin on Ada's mother's side came to Kovno from Brazil. He wanted to claim Ada and take her away from the nurse, raise her in São Paulo. Ada cried bitterly, refused to speak to him, hid, ran away to neighbors' homes, had hysterics. At last the nurse told the cousin that she would give up Ada only if one of her parents came, or an aunt, or uncle, or other very close relative and only if Ada agreed to go.

Word of Ada's survival reached her father's sister Toussia in Sumatra, probably through her uncle Shurik, who himself was very young and nearly penniless in Pennsylvania. Ada's aunt survived the war in a Japanese internment camp.

The Japanese interned all foreigners who were stranded in territories under their occupation during the war. Their circumstances were not to be compared to Auschwitz or Dachau, and Jews were not persecuted because they were Jewish. The conditions, nevertheless, were enormously difficult, food and supplies scarce, and mortality from malnutrition and from illness soaringly high. After the war she was divorced from her first husband and married a Gentile Belgian diplomat. Toussia wrote warm and loving letters to Ada, sent her packages after she moved with her new husband to Brussels.

At last, secure in her second marriage and recovered from the war, she asked for Ada's custody. Ada and her nurse agreed to the arrangements. Plans were set for Ada's move to Belgium when her aunt became mortally ill and died of cancer while still in her forties. Ada looked away from us, into the darkness of the sea just below the terrace on which we were dining.

And so, Ada said, she remained with her nurse. Life was incredibly hard for her and for the two old women with whom she lived. She had no clothes, nor shoes that fit her. Why my parents and Uncle Benjamin did not know of her predicament is a question without a good answer. Ada told me all this without bitterness in her voice, but her eyes, behind her old-fashioned harlequin-shaped glasses, were not tranquil.

At last, in the early 1950s, Ada said, a rich uncle on her mother's side of the family learned of Ada's survival and wrote from England. Though the possibility of moving to Leeds never came up, he sent money, clothes, shoes and food to her caretakers and to Ada. If there was regret in Ada's heart at not being asked to join his family she never expressed it.

Eddy's comments throughout Ada's story had a different mien. He gesticulated his love and pride in Ada. With his hands and his head, and his voice, he spoke bitterly of hurts he feels Ada has suffered. He is wildly, touchingly protective of his wife.

When she tried to find excuses for the behavior of others, he waved them away, said she's too good, too accepting. He talked in a rapid mixture of Russian, Yiddish, German and Hebrew, for he does not speak English. Walter understood even the Russian, of which he knows but a few words. He did not need to know the language to understand Eddy.

Eddy's own life story makes Jonah's journey to Tarshish seem like a holiday. Hearing it in Jaffa was like listening to a heroic Haftorah, which follows every Torah reading in synagogue on Sabbath.

He, too, was born in Kovno, and his family, too, was incarcerated in the Kovno ghetto in 1941. Like Ada, he was also saved by a Gentile, but in his case it was done for vast sums of money. Eddy does not belittle the heroism of the farm family that hid him. He merely states the exchange of money as fact.

Eddy's parents, and their neighbors in the ghetto, built a secret wall behind which they hid small children during "actions." The little ones were given potent sleeping pills to assure their silence. When German soldiers became suspicious they shot through the walls, killing children while they were asleep.

Eddy was only four, yet he remembers each "action" as if it happened the other day. His voice trembled as he spoke; his face looked chiseled in granite. Before an "action" he refused to swallow the pills. His parents had no choice; they could not force-feed pills down his throat. He learned, however, to be totally still when necessary.

His parents, like Ada's, knew that the end of the ghetto was imminent. Having hidden money and jewels, his father bribed a German soldier and made arrangements to smuggle Eddy out of the ghetto into the home of farmers, who were also handsomely paid.

That day Eddy was fooled into taking a strong sleeping potion. When he became oblivious to the world, Eddy was put in a large porous bag with dried peas. This bag was carefully put on a truck, with dozens of other bags filled with peas and other staples. The German soldier, who accepted money from Eddy's parents, helped load and guard the entire shipment on its way from Kovno to a neighboring town.

Instead of the belly of a whale, Eddy was inside a bag of dried peas. Not for an offense such as Jonah committed.

By prearrangement, and prepayment, the bag was thrown from the truck into the arms of a farm couple who lived along the road on which the truck traveled. Eddy remembers the moment when he woke up in the home of the peasants. He began to howl and wail for his mother. He continued to wail for days, refused to eat, slept in short spurts and only when totally depleted. The farmer's wife had an upright piano; she played it loudly, though how well Eddy could hardly judge or recall. When his cries were piercing enough to raise the suspicions of neighboring farmers, she played it for hours. There isn't enough money in the world to repay such a heroic fulfillment of the commitment the farming couple made to Eddy's parents.

As often happened, Eddy got used to his fate. He trotted, barefoot, after his "uncle" and "auntie," helped them in the fields, in the barn and the yard. He recalled that the soles of his feet felt like leather.

The farming couple gave Eddy a small cross. He kissed it each morning and every evening and acted like a Gentile child, though his keepers did not baptize or convert him to their Christian faith.

When the war ended, Eddy's father appeared at the farm as if he were a mirage. He survived Dachau. When he approached Eddy, his son ran away. He still remembers kissing his cross, calling his own father all manner of anti-Semitic names. It was, he reflected in Jaffa, the means of remaining an ingratiating presence in his new family's life, a way of being part of their fabric. He wanted to belong, to feel safe, to be considered a son. They expressed similar anti-Semitic sentiments while hiding Eddy—either to be considered safe from authorities and neighbors, or because these were their true feelings. Eddy wasn't taking a chance.

In fact, Eddy took no chances for a long, long time. He kept the cross hidden in a pocket, just in case the enemy came and he had to prove that he was not a Jew. For years many children hidden by Gentiles carried crosses, false baptismal papers and religious medals—proof that they had a "right to life," even when it was no longer needed.

Eddy's father did not insist on taking him away from the

farm. Instead he remained nearby and came to visit Eddy every day, slowly regaining Eddy's trust, hoping to reawaken feelings in his son that were deeply buried.

Several months later another miracle occurred. Eddy's mother, survivor of another camp, appeared. She knew, of course, where to look for Eddy and found both her son and her husband. Eddy's love and loyalty to his mother did not need to be renurtured. He clung to her and together with her rejoined his father. The family was together, at last. For a while.

Eddy's father, a professional before the war, worked in a bakery immediately afterward. Anti-Semitism was as rampant as it had ever been in Lithuania, Eddy said. I knew it was so in Poland, too. On the train from Siberia, crossing the border, we were greeted with shouts of "Jews, go back where you came from!" even though not every person on the train was Jewish.

As a Jew who survived, Eddy's father could not get a job in keeping with his training. And so he dealt out meager bread rations to those with coupons. One day a man came into the bakery to claim his ration. When he found that there was no bread on the shelves, the man became abusive to Eddy's father, whose patience was wearing thin as well. He answered the irate customer that it was the government's fault, not his, that bread was scarce. He should take himself and his ire to the offices of Kovno's prefecture, not vent it on him. The furious customer reported Eddy's father's words to government authorities, instead of lodging his own justifiable complaint about the shortage of bread.

Eddy's face turned dark. He suspected, but never could

confirm, that the informer was a Jew trying to ingratiate himself with the authorities by reporting his father's careless but truthful remarks.

Eddy's father was immediately arrested and sentenced to many years of hard labor near Archangelsk, in deepest Russia. The man who lived through the Kovno ghetto, and Dachau, was incarcerated within a year or two in the most feared part of the Soviet Union, worse even than the part of Siberia that I knew so well.

But it was so. Eddy's father remained in a labor camp near Archangelsk for five years. Once a year Eddy and his mother were allowed to visit. They traveled for weeks on primitive trains, and at the end of the railroad line they made their way on loading platforms. They stayed in a forsaken hut near the camp. It was impossible to buy anything: food, clothing, firewood. That was all Eddy told us. We could fill in the details. We'd read Solzhenitzyn and Sharansky.

After Stalin died, Eddy's father was "rehabilitated" and permitted to leave. He returned to Kovno and a degree of normalcy entered their lives.

Eddy and Ada knew each other for years, first in the Kovno ghetto where they lived in the same narrow alley. That, of course, they did not remember. Eddy's parents did. Later Eddy saw Ada in high school, but she kept company with another young man. The last series of brief encounters, then longer meetings, then dates, then more, culminated in marriage while they were in medical school in Kovno. Eddy is a dentist and Ada an internist.

Ada's nanny was thrilled that Ada married a Jew. She

felt this would have pleased her parents; they could rest easier in their unknown graves, knowing that Ada's husband had her ancestors' faith, too.

Ada and Eddy worked hard in their professions in Kovno. They had a son, named Liova for Ada's father, they helped support Eddy's parents whose health was frail, and took care of the old nurse and her sister, the only "parents" Ada knew. Despite a tolerable existence, they decided to seek an openly Jewish life and applied for exit visas to Israel. In the 1970s it was not a decision to be made lightly. They succeeded and, as if by a magic wand, they also got permission to take some of their belongings, most important their treasured books.

Eddy's parents were allowed to emigrate, too. Ada's nanny could not leave her very old sister, although both Ada and Eddy urged them to seek visas. Eddy's father and Ada's nanny recently died. Both are mourned, equally, for both were parents.

Life was hard when they arrived in Israel, but when they were both forty, they had another son whose name is Daniel. A native Israeli, a real Sabra. Eddy says that life is still hard; Ada is gentler in assessing their life in Natanya. Though her schedule is grueling and her pay as a physician in the state health care system quite unsubstantial, she feels they live well. She says that she has all she really needs. She even learned to drive at age forty-seven and bought an old mini-Morris automobile. She laughed: "I've got to lose weight or soon I won't fit behind the wheel!"

Ada is plump, but it is very becoming. Her sunny face is completely unwrinkled, though she'd just marked her fiftieth birthday. Walter pronounced Ada absolutely adorable. *Adorable* is the perfect word for Ada. When I said that a sick person would get immediately better from her smile, and her touch, and her young and melodious voice, Ada smiled with obvious pleasure.

Eddy said that doctors are not really respected in Israel, not as they are in Europe. But, he quickly added, with a Moroccan click of the tongue, he could not imagine living anywhere else. They'd just returned from a two-week holiday in Europe, their first in ten years, taken instead of renovating their crumbling apartment in Natanya.

At the airport in Zurich, Eddy said, he felt immediately at home when he joined the line of passengers going to Israel. His *neshomah*, his soul, was at ease in the El Al line. Those were his words: his *neshomah* was at ease as soon as he was with his own people.

Ada nodded in passionate agreement. That was how she felt in the El Al line at the airport in Zurich, how she feels every day in Israel. Despite constant danger and anxiety, despite problems and unrest in the land, Ada's and Eddy's *neshomah*s, their souls, which have seen so much sorrow, are at peace.

Alik

Alik is unable to admit that people do nice things for one another. He questions motives and actions. He minimizes his own noble deeds—of which there are many—and grimaces at the good intentions of others. I called him a cynic during one of our visits in Jerusalem. He recoiled, as if I'd stung him. I asked "why" of him and myself.

"It upset me," he snapped, "because *you* said it." Sign, perhaps, that he valued my opinion. Instead of feeling complimented I was guilt-ridden.

Alik was saved by a Nazi soldier during a death march at the end of World War II. Cynicism, I thought, would be alien to his very existence. Yet who's to judge, and I did—and was wrong. Alik is not really a cynic.

Alik's parents and mine knew one another in Vilna. Alik is his childhood nickname; that's how I think of him and that's what I call him. His formal name is Alexander. He and I are about the same age, but we met after the war through a song, not in person. He composed it when he was eleven or twelve, incarcerated in the ghetto.

Every survivor of the Holocaust knows it. Grisha and Mira's daughter recalled the melody, though she was only a baby when someone hummed or sang it to her in the Vilna ghetto. Every collection of ghetto songs includes it. It's sung at every memorial observance. It is our dirge. "Quiet, quiet, let's be silent, graves are growing here . . ." Alik's melody, and the poet Schmerke Katcherginsky's words, break the most stalwart hearts.

Alik will not speak of this song, will not be reminded that he wrote it. When he came to visit us in New York for the first time, bursting with energy, kinetic movement, bravura, I said something about it. I'd just sung it at a memorial service for the Vilna ghetto. He brushed off my references to Vilna, to his song, to the past. Not just with impatience, a wave of the hand, but with a bang on the coffee table. I never mentioned it to him again, but I can't help thinking of it. Years later, however, he spoke of it briefly in a film about the partisans of Vilna.

I heard a lecture once about the daily life of the Vilna ghetto. The speaker said that in his mind nothing loomed larger than the heroism of men and women who tried to keep day-to-day life in the ghetto "normal." Every person who taught the Aleph-Bet-Gimmel-Dalet, the Yiddish-Hebrew alphabet, in the midst of destruction, was a hero.

Mama's cousins and others had told me that the ghetto organized a theater group and had a small orchestra, which changed daily as participants died or disappeared. My uncle Liusik played the violin with the group. Music lessons were given, contests were held. Alik's song was the winner of just such a competition. Heroism comes in various guises. It assures our survival as a people.

Alik says that he does not care about Vilna, doesn't wish to remember it. His good memories ended when he and his father were trapped like animals on a ghetto street during an "action." His father thrust Alik into the arms of a friend, a doctor who was being led to a truck for deportation. How did his father know that the truck would not be going to Ponar? Why did the guards permit Alik's father to hand him over to another man? These are the miracles by which some people were saved and others were not.

Alik struggled fiercely with his father's friend. He hit and pummeled the doctor's chest. He tried desperately to return to his father, but the man held Alik in a tight grip until the truck moved away and he could no longer jump out. That was the last time Alik saw his father.

The truck took the victims to Stutthof, a concentration camp where people died all around Alik. The doctor in whose arms Alik struggled became deathly ill. The boy refused to eat his rations so the doctor might have a bit more sustenance.

One day, as the Allied forces began overtaking the Nazis, the camp commandant ordered all inmates to gather at the gate. They would be led away from advancing Allied troops. Such death marches were common. The emaciated marchers walked for days under the pointed guns of their tormentors. Anyone who fell was shot on the spot.

Alik fell during the march. He remembers the Nazi guard hesitating for a split second. In that moment he must have felt pity; instead of shooting him, the S.S. man grabbed Alik by the collar and shoved him into a clump of bushes by the roadside. He lay motionless until everyone passed him; then he slept for hours. When he awoke, he decided to walk with no idea where the back roads would lead him.

Another miracle happened to Alik: he crossed the Swiss border without being stopped by police. Villagers along the way helped him. Once he reached a large city, he was put in touch, by the Red Cross or a Jewish organization, with his paternal grandmother who'd lived for years in Tel Aviv. He was given food and lodging and later he received money from them for passage to Palestine, where he joined her.

Radio was the lifeline for survivors of World War II. People sent in their names and listened to programs that gave the names of other survivors. Thus families, sometimes, found one another. Alik's name was heard in Paris after the war by someone who knew that his mother had escaped death, too. She learned that Alik was in Tel Aviv. She joined him there as soon as she was able to obtain a visa; no easy matter for survivors of the Holocaust.

Alik's mother told me their full story in 1988, matter-of-factly, without tears or histrionics. Alik will not talk about it. His life, he says, began when he reached the Holy Land and went to the conservatory in Jerusalem. His mother says it is true, that is when his life truly began.

After Alik graduated, he became a concert pianist and teamed up with Bracha, another young musician who was a fellow student at the conservatory. They are the preeminent duo-piano team in Israel and play all over the world. Bracha is married—not to Alik—and has a son and two grand-children. Her husband and Alik behave like brothers. Alik dotes on their family. He has many students, many friends, and always some huge, slobbering dog who adores him.

He and Bracha are now, very occasionally, composers in tandem. They "composed" a diabolically clever piece for two pianos and electronic instruments, which was praised for its virtuosity not only by critics in Israel, but in Europe as well. Few knew that this was a parody of modern music, a joke Alik and Bracha played on the critics and public. One of the musical instruments was a Keren Kayemet *pushke,* the blue Jewish National Fund charity box found in many Jewish kitchens. Bracha's young son shook it along with`pots and pans and other alarming noisemakers. That same participant in the electronic-instrument ensemble made other sounds for the musical offering, best left un-described.

In the strange way of the world we found out that Walter knew Bracha's family when he arrived in Jerusalem from Vienna in the 1930s, and that he had had a crush on her older sister before he emigrated to America in 1939 to rejoin his family. He was a student at the same conservatory where Alik and Bracha studied later. My meeting Bracha and Walter's meeting Alik was like a circle coming to completion. Each one of us knew the other in another life and now we all know each other in our lives together.

We spent a lot of time with Alik, Bracha and the families during our two visits in Israel in 1988. Alik's home is in Ein Kerem; Bracha's in the center of Jerusalem. Ein Kerem is mentioned in the Bible; it has many Christian and Jewish holy places. Now it also has a huge and bustling annex of Hadassah Hospital— a typical juxtaposition in Israel. Many artists live there, too. Alik lives in an art center, in rooms immediately adjoining the concert hall, where many recitals, lectures and other cultural activities take place. He and Bracha's family bought the building when it was on the verge of falling down, and they restored it to its present beauty with help from others. The families spend Sabbath there together: Alik, his mother, Bracha and her brood, guests, relatives, students.

Walter and I went to Alik's house for our first Sabbath eve dinner in Israel in the spring of 1988, while we were staying at Mishkenot Sha'ananim. Bracha and her family, of course, were there. Alik's mother came from Tel Aviv, as she normally comes for Sabbath. Fenia is a small, compact, lively and loquacious woman, with keen insights. She is almost totally blind.

Although she and I never met before as adults, we took to each other in Israel as ducks do to water. Our pond was filled with memories of Vilna. Fenia was telling me stories of the good old days as if I were Alik.

While washing dishes together, I noticed that she wore just the kind of apron I wanted to buy in Jerusalem. It looked like Mama's and Grandmother's aprons in Vilna. She told me she'd gotten it in Australia, when she went to visit the doctor who saved Alik's life. He survived that march too, and now made his home in Melbourne. She only bought the apron because it resembled her aprons in the Jerusalem of Lithuania. "You'll never find one in Jerusalem," she laughed.

Except when one is with Alik, a small reference to Vilna

will lead the natives to a cascade of stories, a veritable can-you-top-this contest. As I was wiping plates, glasses and silver, I asked whether she knew the Vilna kidnapping story. She insisted I tell her, yet I suspect she knew it herself. It did not take much to persuade me, though there is a wonderful version of it in Yiddish in a book by A. Karpinowicz, published in Israel.

Two men arrived from America in the late 1920s or early 1930s to connect with Vilna's *Unterwelt Menschen* (underworld people, petty criminals) to plan the kidnapping of the child of a rich merchant. When the plan was completed and the evil scheme carried out, the American gangsters, with the help of their Vilna henchmen, brought the boy to the home of one of the criminals in Vilna. When they handed the boy to the henchman's wife, she realized what was afoot and screamed at her husband and his accomplices that this was a child from a family of means, that he was surely used to cocoa and sweet rolls for supper, to a soft bed with a down blanket, to warm, new pajamas—none of which she possessed. She bullied the men to buy forthwith all the things she deemed necessary to keep the child as comfortable as possible under the dire circumstances. When they returned and she had fed, bathed and tucked the child into bed, she proceeded to yell at her husband and his cohorts about their heinous deed. She screamed and cursed them throughout the evening and all night too.

The next morning the Vilna criminals announced to their American "partners" that they should pack their bags and leave as quickly as possible. Kidnappings were not a fitting business for criminals in Vilna. They would not perform such deeds in our town! The American criminals departed, the *Unterwelt Menschen* telephoned the frantic family, and returned their son, in his brand new pajamas, wrapped in a down blanket, and very well fed.

Fenia agreed that it was a marvelous, yet terrifying, story, but she would tell me a better one, and it happened to her! My dish-wiping speed came to a near halt; I was afraid that if we finished our task and went back to the table, she'd either shorten her tale or have it dismissed by her son with his customary impatience. I murmured several times, *"Nu?"* meaning "So? Go on . . ." to prime the pump of her well of recollections.

Her husband and she moved to a new apartment in Vilna, when Alik was about eighteen months old. All the furniture was moved by professionals, and most of their personal belongings were in the truck as well. However, she packed a large separate suitcase with Alik's new baby clothes. Since she had a set of valuable and cherished antique crystal cups and saucers, and a tureenlike bowl, she wrapped them carefully in cotton and soft paper and nestled them among Alik's things.

The suitcase was stolen in the move. The thieves obviously knew the family and where their new home was going to be. A ransom letter duly arrived. This, according to Fenia, was not so rare an event even in Vilna. She said that we had common thieves with names like Srulke the Ganef (Srulke the Thief), who most certainly were not in league with Al Capone or John Dillinger.

In any event, the ransom letter set a time and place for negotiations in Novogorod, the most unsavory district in

Vilna. Fenia decided to handle the matter herself. My *"Nu?"* became "NO!" She wasn't afraid, she said, to go to a particular courtyard in the evening to meet Vilna thieves. After all, they weren't American gangsters! I didn't ask why her husband or another male member of the family did not go in her stead. Women in Vilna were liberated and did everything, including meeting thieves in dark courtyards.

The negotiator was waiting when she arrived. She recognized his face. A common thief, not one to be taken too seriously. He proposed the sum of one hundred fifty zloty for the return of her suitcase. She said it was too much for baby clothes. "Ah," the thief declared, "you have some very fine crystal among the clothing." She bargained until they agreed on one hundred twenty zloty, shook hands on the deal and agreed on the time when she would pay the ransom.

After money changed hands, a young boy brought her the suitcase. With it he handed her a ten-zloty bill. When she asked why she was getting this money, he hung his head and told her that one of her cups was inadvertently broken. They could not keep the whole sum they'd agreed on.

"So," she asked, "did you ever hear of thieves like that anywhere but in Vilna? And this isn't just a *meise,* a story, it really happened to me in 1932."

"Does Alik know it?" I asked.

"No." She shrugged. "He wouldn't care."

We returned to the dinner table, where the talk was of the difficult political situation in Israel, of candidates and elections, of imposssible choices. Everyone was speaking at top volume in four or five different languages. I am ashamed to admit that I'd have preferred to stay in the kitchen to hear more stories in Yiddish about long ago and far away.

When it was time to return to Mishkenot Sha'ananim, Alik insisted on driving us back. The night was clear, the moon so near, so light, so full, that if I were tall enough, I'd have reached up and taken it down and sent it to my children back in New York.

When we got out in the parking lot, overlooking the Old City, with David's Citadel illuminated against the sky, I put my arm around Alik. "Listen," I said, in Yiddish, "did you ever hear the story of your stolen baby clothes in Vilna?"

"Go away," Alik muttered. "Who cares about old clothes in Vilna?"

"Well, Alik, I'm going to tell you anyway." Alik stood still and listened raptly, his arm relaxed under mine. Because the moon was so bright I could see Alik's eyes behind his thick glasses. They didn't dart nervously in every direction, his face wasn't creased with irritable wrinkles. He looked years younger, lighter in spirit, almost serene. When I finished his mother's story, he laughed. Wonderful, infectious, long-lasting laughter. It rose and fell, and rose again like waves in the sea. I can hardly recall when laughing with someone brought me such joy. He held me close in a crushing bear hug. *"Nu?"* he said. "Only in Vilna! Only in Vilna," he repeated and laughed. "Only in Vilna could such robberies happen!"

A true cynic would not have had such a reaction.

Lara and Sasha

Sasha's first wife, Zina, whom he loved passionately since early youth, died when a stray bullet hit her. It killed her instantly the day after Vilna was liberated by the Soviet army from the Germans, at the very end of World War II. Some details and all the names here are fictitious, but the story is not.

Sasha had hidden his young wife and baby daughter in an attic, in an abandoned building on the outskirts of the city. As a member of the partisan army, which lurked in the surrounding countryside and killed the enemy whenever possible, he knew the territory well. He prepared their hiding place with as much care and deliberation as if he were planning the advance of the Second Byelorussian Front under General Rokosovsky, or at least as diligently as the partisans planned their forays into enemy strongholds.

He had some non-Jewish contacts in the underground as well, and he was, by nature, an incredibly inventive, clever man. Furthermore, he made equally heroic provisions so that his wife's sister, and her little boy, also members of a partisan group, could stay in another wing of the abandoned building during the last days of World War II. He thought it best not to have two young children in the same quarters. Their noise, controllable with one, would have become unmanageable and dangerous with two.

When the Soviet army stormed, and then occupied, Vilna, the foundation of the abandoned building in which they all hid must have weakened. While no direct bombs hit it, the tremors affected its precarious balance. The day after the bombing and shelling seemed to stop, the wing of the building in which Zina's sister and her son still hid, collapsed.

Zina, hearing the noise, and seeing the collapse through cracks in the wall of her secret room, rushed out into the courtyard. Sasha could not stop her. He had to protect their little child from harm, could not run after Zina to aid her sister.

A Soviet soldier, somewhere close to the abandoned building, did not realize that the running noises and cries of anguish he had overheard came from an unarmed woman, miraculously spared death at the hand of Nazis. That she was scurrying across the courtyard to save her sister from the ruins of the collapsed wing. He released a barrage of bullets. One of these hit and killed Sasha's beloved.

When he saw Zina falling to the ground, he grabbed their child and ran to help her. She was beyond help. The Soviet soldier, seeing the tragedy he so inadvertently caused, and hearing disconnected, nearly hysterical bits of story, ran with Sasha and the little girl, to the collapsed building. They tried to dig out Zina's sister. Her body was finally found, over her son's. The boy was still breathing beneath his mother.

Sasha was left alone to bury two young women: Zina, his wife, best friend, comrade-in-arms in the partisan army, mother of his child. The other his cherished wife's sister. Two small children and he were left alone in the ruins of their native city.

He nearly lost his mind. To have survived the Holocaust, to have served in the partisans together with his wife and child, sister-in-law and nephew, and then to have lost Zina in such a senseless, cruel way almost killed him too. But there were two small children to look after, to feed and to comfort. He knew he had to persevere.

To stay in Vilna, however, became untenable. No other members of his or Zina's families were spared from death. To get out seemed impossible. He had no legal grounds for obtaining visas for Poland, which was the closest "foreign" country to Vilna. No relatives abroad who would send him affidavits to get out of Soviet Lithuania, of which Vilna was once more the capital in 1945.

Someone he knew suggested that he get married, pro forma, to any woman who could get him and the children out of Lithuania, someone who might have the legal wherewithal to help him start a new life. After the war such unions were not uncommon and their basis not always financial. People married and divorced for practical purposes, sometimes for money, but as often for altruistic reasons. I knew of several such marriages—one even while I was still in Siberia.

A search for the right person began.

Lara, also a survivor, was a stranger in Vilna; she was from a neighboring Baltic country where she was interned in a small concentration camp, without gas chambers. People died there of starvation, typhoid, other dread diseases and by hanging or shooting. A "safer" concentration camp.

She was married and divorced before the war began. Her first husband and she parted cordially; he left Estonia for South Africa in 1939. She wrote to him when the war ended. He responded immediately, sent generous gifts of money, clothing, food, staples; offered whatever other help she might require.

Lara was a gorgeous woman. Tall, elegant, haughty, with lovely auburn hair and slightly protruding, piercingly blue eyes. A lady.

She asked her first husband to arrange for an affidavit for her to leave Vilna for Lodz, Poland, ostensibly later still for Capetown, South Africa. To assuage any fears on his part that she might really arrive and disrupt his life, Lara made it clear that she intended to go from Lodz to Palestine where one of her distant relatives was the wife of Chaim Weizmann, the famous scientist and later first president of the State of Israel. Lara's former husband sent all necessary documents and money to expedite the journey.

Lara, however, was all alone, and fearful of undertaking a move to an unknown place, in need of emotional and physical support and help on her trip to Poland. A meeting between Sasha and Lara was arranged by someone who knew them both. An agreement was reached. Sasha and Lara would marry, she would ask that his name and those of the two children be added to her affidavit and that they would all travel together to Lodz. Once there, he promised that he would help her get settled, look after her affairs. Settle himself and the two children, too. Maybe go back to school, get a degree in engineering, find a niche in life again. Get divorced.

Lara and Sasha went through a marriage ceremony. I knew that and nothing else. They left Vilna in 1946, with Sasha's daughter and little nephew, and came to Lodz where I met them together for the first time.

I knew Sasha before the war, in the 1930s in Vilna, when I was a little girl and he the chief accountant and my father's right hand in the family business. He was, aside from my father and grandfather, the most handsome man I ever knew. I thought he looked like Prince Charming should look in all the fairy tales I adored.

Tall, with wavy brown hair, laughing gray eyes and very bushy eyebrows. I especially liked his eyebrows: they'd rise when he teased me, which he did often, and come close together when he laughed, which he did even more often and with great gusto.

He was also the only man I knew who typed. During particularly frantic times in my father's business, he'd suggest that Sasha take his typewriter and use the study in our house to get his work done. Sasha's hands would fly over the keys. Sometimes I expected music to come out of the machine—he looked so much like Claudio Arrau (who played many concerts in Vilna when I was a child) bent

over a little, peculiarly shaped piano. My day was made
when Sasha put me on his lap and guided my fingers over
the keys. It was like magic.

Sasha and Lara made an extraordinarily handsome couple
when I met them in Lodz in 1946. When they talked to
each other, and to others, too, both seemed tense. Even I,
at nearly sixteen and quite self-involved, noticed something
deeply askew in their relationship. I did not know what it
was, nor ever asked my parents. It was unseemly, far too
intimate, inappropriate to discuss, even with my mother.
Especially with my mother. But I wondered.

Lara was strict with the children; they seemed scared of
her, or at least uneasy in her presence. When his daughter
and nephew were alone with Sasha and I met them by chance
on the street, or when he brought only them to visit, they
were easier in spirit, smiling, friendly.

A year went by. Lara and Sasha did not go their separate
ways. They lived together. The pro forma marriage seemed
to become a formal union. Sasha went to college, got a
degree in civil engineering and worked as well.

We left Lodz for Sweden in 1947, later for America
from Stockholm. He and Lara went to Israel, together, with
the children. He got a good job; the country needed en-
gineers. We gathered from letters my father and Sasha
exchanged regularly that they settled into a normal life.

I saw them on visits to Israel; so did my mother and my
father. My daughter met Sasha in 1968, when she and I
took a trip together to see the Holy Land. At nearly twelve,
she thought him as handsome as I did at five or six. Many
more years went by. We all got older, though when my

father was eighty-eight he still referred to Sasha as that "good, good boy." The good, good boy turned seventy-seven that spring.

Before we saw Lara and Sasha again in Israel, in April of 1988, I asked about them of mutual friends, people who know them intimately, live in close proximity, see each other often. I was no longer held back by a postwar teenager's self-involvement and shyness, and my questions were not addressed to my very private, reticent mother.

My friends, their friends too, eagerly answered all the questions I asked; offered even more information than I really wanted. Some things are better left unspoken, guessed at, rather than confirmed. What happened, my friends said, was that Lara fell madly in love with Sasha *after* the pro forma marriage was arranged. Sasha did not return her love and made no secret of it, ever. He told Lara that he had had one true love, did not want or need another. She hoped that with time he'd change his mind. To go through a divorce by then was unthinkable to her.

Sasha must have realized—though that I was not told and am merely surmising—what difficulties a contested divorce would bring down on all their heads. He stayed with Lara, but he never loved her and did not hide it. He refused to have a child with her; a bitter, cruel disappointment in her life. She tended and disciplined Sasha's daughter and nephew carefully, but if she had love for them in her heart, it was hidden from them and Sasha, too. From everyone around them as well. Revenge, perhaps, or a true lack of feeling for the children.

Sasha's nephew went back to Poland after he came of

age in Israel, married a Gentile girl, lives in Cracow, seldom writes and never visits. His daughter married very young, had a baby, divorced soon after, brought up her daughter by herself. Sasha helped while Lara remained distant and by all accounts correct. A real lady.

While staying in Jerusalem in the spring of 1988, I telephoned Sasha and Lara a number of times. Each time we spoke, Lara made every decision on how, when and where we should meet. Sasha was eager to see Mishkenot Sha'ananim, the artists' colony near Moses Montefiore's famous windmill, where we stayed. Lara changed every plan. Sasha called her the Chief. To me, I told him, he'd always been the Chief and always would be, but nothing could be arranged without Lara's imprimatur.

Finally we did meet, not at Mishkenot. I had not seen either one of them for more than a decade, too long a time to let slip by without seeing important people from one's childhood and memory bank.

Both Sasha and Lara looked elegant and composed. She cool and commanding, with snow-white, beautifully cut hair, and the same, slightly bulging, but still piercingly blue eyes. Perhaps a somewhat sadder, and kinder, woman than I remembered from years before. His eyebrows as dark and bushy as ever, though his still abundant, wavy hair had turned steel gray, the color of his immaculately tailored suit and expensive silk tie.

We talked of their semiretired life overlooking a quiet harbor, the children, my father, his daughter and granddaughter, who was about to become a surgeon. Sasha's nephew was briefly mentioned, his daughter's and granddaughter's accomplishments lauded while we were out of Lara's hearing. A polite visit. Lara was more agreeable to me in person than on the telephone, charming, knowledge-able, widely read and well-informed, very pleasant to be with.

Between Lara and Sasha there seems to exist an uneasy truce, a state of well-controlled peace, achieved, no doubt, at enormous emotional expense. Whether the result has been worth the price both have surely paid over the years is only for them to know and to judge.

Katya

This brief story of a long and
difficult life was told to me
in short, isolated chapters by my mother after we came to
America. It is retold here just as I heard it, with only a few
unimportant facts and names changed to avoid pain.

Katya was my mother's friend in Vilna; she was a friend
to many. Her family was very well-to-do. Her husband had
had wide business connections before the war, including
dealings with my father's family firm.

After the war, everyone in my family referred to him
only as Katya's husband, or by his last name: Feller. My
mother never once mentioned his given name. Neither did
Papa, nor mutual friends, nor Katya in the years I knew
her in New York. It was always just Feller, as if he were a
stranger.

She and her husband had had four children in Vilna, two

boys and two girls. Katya was enormously popular; everyone relished her sense of humor, improvisations at the piano, the belting way in which she sang *schlagers,* as popular hits were called in Poland, her general high spirits. She was also very pretty. Not gorgeous, or stunning or beautiful. My mother, who used words carefully and exactly, insisted that *pretty* was the word that best described Katya in her youth.

Katya's husband had dealings not only with businesses in Vilna, but with firms abroad. Not long before the war began in 1939 he had to go to South America to see some clients. Despite the fact that times were uncertain, he decided to pursue his business ventures. He left Vilna owing my father a rather large sum of money. Perhaps he owed money to others, too.

Feller recently died, a very old man. Even after his death, the debt came up when Papa and I talked about Feller. "The man could have easily repaid it. He was a rich man! Where was his honor? Perhaps honorable instincts were not second nature to Feller," Papa muttered with contempt.

"Perhaps he'd forgotten his debt," Mama used to say before she died. Papa remembers the exact sum Feller owed him. The equivalent of thirty-eight hundred dollars in Poland before the war; a considerable sum in 1939, a considerable sum afterward too. The fact that Feller never even mentioned it to Papa after the war, either by letter or in person when they met once in New York, seems to bother him more than the loss of money.

When the war broke out, Katya's husband was still in South America. He could not come back to Vilna. Katya and their children could not join him. The family was split apart, isolated from one another. After Vilna fell to German forces, letters ceased coming as well.

During the Nazi terror annihilating Vilna, nearly all of Katya's family was wiped out. Only she and one daughter were saved. I had heard of their wartime experience from Mama, who'd heard it from Katya, and from one of my mother's cousins. They were together in a "good" concentration camp in one of the Baltic countries, without gas chambers.

After the war Katya wrote to her husband, or perhaps she sent him a telegram, or maybe a Jewish agency put them in touch. I could ascertain the details by asking how they connected, but they are not worth the pain they might cause people who know what they are.

Affidavits, money, tickets, all that wealth and political pull could bring, Feller provided to Katya and their only surviving child. He accumulated them in abundance while his family was being destroyed during the war. She and their daughter left Europe in style, long before many of the other survivors could leave war-torn Warsaw.

When Katya and her twenty-year-old daughter arrived in South America, they discovered that their generous, loving husband and father had a second wife and another, very young daughter. Katya was crazed with anger, disillusionment, jealousy, outrage. How dare he? While she and the rest of the family were in agony, or dying, or dead, he fell in love again, married, had a child and prospered?

Katya's husband was undoubtedly distraught as well. Since my sympathy was not with his predicament, I seldom, if ever, considered his feelings. Feller, to me, was on the next to the lowest rung on the ladder of *menschlichkeit,* the Yiddish word that encompasses humanity: people's behavior and common decency. I was only seventeen when I first heard this family's fate. It was easy to make severe judgments then. Now it is harder.

Years later Mama told me that Feller had proposed a plan to Katya. I am sure that it was one of the very few times in her life when she repeated a confidence relayed to her by a friend. She did it without comment, or any opinion. Feller had offered to set up his second wife and their child in a *casa chica,* or small house, an arrangement not uncommon among wealthy families in his new homeland. Many men had such agreements with their wives.

Katya and her daughter would be installed in the *casa grande,* the family's main residence—elegant, large, official. A fierce and proud Katya would not agree to such a travesty. It was to be either a complete break with his second family or she would have nothing to do with Feller. She did not need him; she did not want him on those terms.

However, as life turned out, she did need him. She would need him more and more as time went by. Katya and her daughter came to a land where they did not know the language. They had no friends. They were not in New York or Tel Aviv, or even in Buenos Aires or Rio de Janeiro. They were in a small, provincial town, in an isolated, underdeveloped country. They had no stature in the community. To the local families they were interlopers, disturbing the rhythm of their placid lives. One of their own had married Feller, had a child, belonged.

Katya and her daughter settled in a small house for which

Feller, naturally, paid. They accepted a monthly, or weekly, allowance to buy food, clothing, pay doctors' bills, schooling for the young woman. After several years of this intolerable situation for everyone concerned, including the second wife and young child, Katya and her daughter moved away from the small South American town and came to New York.

When Katya met my mother again, on the Upper West Side of New York where we all lived within blocks of one another, they spent time together in person and in long conversations over the telephone. They reminisced about their days in Vilna, about afternoon tea at Stral's Café, about their mutual friends, most of whom did not survive the war, about their current lives.

The day came when Katya, older and frail, told Mama that maybe she'd acted like a vain and proud fool when she refused Feller's plan right after the war. Perhaps she should have moved into the *casa grande* with her daughter, become the lady of the domain, looked away from the rest of her terrible situation? She might still have had some good years to sing, to dance, to enjoy life. What did she accomplish by being proud?

I asked my astute, razor-sharp, incredibly sensitive mother, more than once, what she would have had Katya do. Not what she would have done herself under similar circumstances. Between us that would have been an intrusive question.

I almost always got straight answers when I asked questions of Mama. She knew her own mind and spoke it. In this case she wavered, she sighed, she floundered. I was astonished and looked it, but she would not become judge and jury of this situation. In some respects, she'd say slowly, it was unthinkable. In others, said even more slowly, she could not say. "Those who cannot accept their own frailties are less able to understand them in others." Having said that much, she'd sigh heavily, light another of her endless chain of cigarettes, inhale deeply, become distracted and blow smoke through her nostrils.

I do not know whether Katya and her husband ever went through a formal divorce. His second wife was not Jewish, so his first marriage did not matter in the eyes of her church. It certainly made no difference to Katya.

Feller did not stint to make Katya's life comfortable. She had a nice, though hardly luxurious, apartment one block away from ours. I used to see her often on the street. Sometimes she wore a mink coat, incongruous on the tiny, frail, sad lady. There were no signs, either in her bearing or on her face, of the young woman Mama told me about. Katya, who sang and danced and told terrific jokes in Vilna, disappeared, not only in the ghetto and concentration camps in Europe, but in the small town in South America to which she came to build life anew.

When Katya's health failed completely to chronic disease, she moved in with her daughter and her family, close to her old home and ours. Her daughter married a nice man who came to America before the war started. They had two children. One of them was a good friend of one of my children. They attended elementary school together in our neighborhood. I am not sure how much of her family history my daughter's friend knew. Nothing was ever mentioned in our house about it and so my daughter never asked a single question.

As the years went along, Katya's daughter became quite friendly with her father's wife and her much younger half sister. The half sister, and her mother, went with Katya's daughter to Israel while Katya was left in the care of nurses in New York. I can only guess at my mama's reaction, for she was dead by the time this trip took place.

I'd heard, though not directly from Katya's daughter, that her visits and contact with her father and his second family increased even further after Katya died. The relationship became close and deeply intertwined, whatever its reasons, though I suspect that some were financial, not purely filial or based only on love.

If only Mama were here to help me put in proper perspective the dark thoughts about this unhappy story that I still harbor in back of my mind.

Mrs. S.

She has snow-white hair, always beautifully arranged and becoming to her features. Her eyeglasses enhance her face, and give sparkle to her gaze. Without them her eyes lack focus; one is somewhat smaller than the other and has a slight cast to it. In her case, even glasses add to her charm.

Her skin is barely wrinkled, younger than her eighty-one years on this planet might warrant. It has shielded her face without getting a lift. Except from inside.

She wears vivid colors—green, red, bright blue, violet, magenta and purple. Her beads and earrings are equally bright, large and very becoming.

Papa, who lives in the same building as she does in Florida, says it is a pleasure to be with her. She is stylish, charming, vivacious and always in a good mood.

What I remember best about her, though, is her high,

girlish, exuberant voice, whatever the language she uses to communicate her zest for life. Speaking to her over the telephone makes one feel she is only in her twenties, possibly thirties. Certainly not an octogenarian voice. Perhaps its joyous timbre, clarity and carrying power have been enhanced by her lifelong love for choral singing. Even in her eighties, Mrs. S. sings in a community choir in Miami Beach.

Mrs. S. was born and grew up in Cracow, a beautiful and historic city in the heart of Poland. Its university, library, museums and churches were famous, still are, not just in Poland, but throughout Europe. Polish nobility has a long history in Cracow; so has the Catholic Church. Pope John Paul II is a native.

She speaks a classically beautiful Polish, unencumbered by regional accents, intonation or dialect. Her Yiddish is spoken with a Galician accent; "foreign" to someone from Vilna and other regions near my hometown. If her Polish is classic, then so is our Yiddish. In others I find the Galician way of speaking my favorite language somewhat annoying. It is not the way it was written by I. L. Peretz and Sholem Aleichem. When Mrs. S. speaks it, the sound is perfectly charming and absolutely right. It must be her voice.

She married for the first time during the 1930s, in Cracow. Her husband was a physician, from a prominent and wealthy family. They had one son, an extremely bright and talented child. A veritable *wunderkind* in his grasp of mathematics and science. Mrs. S. told me so, and I believe her; she does not seem prone to motherly exaggerations.

When the Second World War began and the Germans

spread their destruction eastward, Mrs. S., her husband and son moved eastward still farther, to Vilna. They hoped to escape the German tentacles strangling Cracow.

In Vilna the boy was enrolled in the same school, Epstein's Gymnasium, to which some of my cousins and other relatives went. Mrs. S. was not, still is not, a Yiddishist who would have been drawn to the schools that my mother in her youth, and I in my childhood, had attended in Vilna.

Her husband was able to work and provide for their needs, perhaps not as well as he did in Cracow, but they managed. She never mentioned that their housing in Vilna during those difficult days, when many refugees started to seek homes in my city, was inadequate or cramped or unpleasant. That may be due to her temperament rather than the reality of their situation. I know it was a terrible problem for others.

Soon, however, her husband and Mrs. S. realized that the Germans could not be contained, that no matter how far east of Cracow they'd run, the Germans would eventually follow and destroy them. During their stay in Vilna, they'd heard remarkable news of a Japanese consul in Kovno, Lithuania. Senpo Sugihara, Mrs. S. told me in Florida fifty years later, was, in her opinion, another Raoul Wallenberg. He was stamping the passports of unfortunate Jews with visas for entry to Japan, to so-called freedom. Other people, including my mother's cousins, also knew of this remarkable road to escape from Europe, but they were afraid that it might be some sort of trap, that their trip to Japan, via the Trans-Siberian railroad and a boat from Vladivostok to Kobe, would land them instead in the Gulag nightmare of

Stalin's Russia. Everyone with Japanese transit visas also had to receive permission from the dreaded NKVD (the secret police of the Soviet Union) in order to travel from Vilna to Vladivostok.

Mrs. S. and her husband had no such fears. They went to Kovno in pursuit of visas to Japan. Consul Sugihara granted them permission. He did this, by all accounts, out of moral conviction, without official sanction or permission from his superiors. Even as he was being transferred by the Japanese government to another post in war-torn Europe, Consul Sugihara was issuing transit visas on his way to the railroad station, and even in the railroad car before the train began moving.

Mrs. S.'s story seemed to come from another planet. Yet once heard it reached me from other directions as well. Looking through a spring 1989 issue of the *Jewish Week* in New York, many months after visiting with Mrs. S. in Miami, I noticed that the "Courage to Care Award" was to be given to Consul Sugihara. I went to the ceremony at the Anti-Defamation League of B'nai B'rith and met the late consul's wife and son, who had been with him in Kovno. I told them of Mrs. S., and of her continuing gratitude and admiration for the man she considers a true hero. I learned that he is the only Japanese honored with a tree and a plaque on the Avenue of the Righteous Gentiles in Yad Vashem in Jerusalem, and that one of his sons and a grandson live and work part of each year in Israel.

In Mrs. S.'s words, their escape from Europe to what she thought would be a safe harbor in Japan was quite unforgettable. Her demeanor, her voice, her enthusiasm in recalling that time was almost romantic. It was a reckless adventure, not a flight for life. Why, she said, the trip from Kovno back to Vilna, and then on the Trans-Siberian railroad all the way to Vladivostok was marvelous.

Others who'd taken that trip do not recall it as does Mrs. S. They do not possess her wonderful nature—her glass of tea was always half full, not half empty. The samovar was going all day long in the dining car of the train. It was warm and cozy, her husband and son were with her. They were on their way to safety, or so they believed. Life was going to be terrific. The *r*'s rolled off like sharp little bells in her Polish-inflected English pronunciation. Behind the glasses, with their becoming pink frames, her eyes glistened.

In Vladivostok they transferred to a boat, which took them to the Japanese port of Kobe. When I asked her about it, she said the boat was dreadful, simply awful, too disagreeable to discuss or remember. And as good as her word, she refused to talk about the discomforts of the crossing. But the arrival in Kobe was another chapter in her long, long life.

Oh, that gorgeous port, the breathtaking countryside, the beauty of Japan! Mrs. S. looked away, into the far reaches of her Florida living room, filled with objets d'art— they were just that, not *tchachkes* and bibelots—and for a moment she seemed wistful, far removed from her home in Miami Beach.

When I told her that my husband played in Kobe many times, that he loved Japan, that he was going again, she was horrified that I'd never gone with him, never seen its beauty and charm. The six months she spent in Kobe are an unforgettable part of her life. She relished the strange new culture of Japan.

Mrs. S. and her family were generously taken care of by the Japanese Jewish community of Kobe. She recalled that in 1940 there were some one hundred Jews, most of them in the import-export business. Before arriving in Kobe in the 1920s or 1930s they had lived in Manchuria, having come there from central Russia and Eastern Europe when the Trans-Siberian Railroad was in its infancy. Most of them were in the textile business, and most of them came to Kobe to take charge of shipping their goods all over the world.

Most of the Kobe Jews spoke Russian, as did the Jews saved by Consul Sugihara's transit visas. In the beginning, the new arrivals from Vilna and Kovno were invited to join the households of these families and treated as relatives. Having no language barrier was enormously comforting.

As the number of refugees increased through Consul Sugihara's humanitarian intervention, the Jewish community found itself strapped. The leaders of the community sent an SOS to the Joint Distribution Committee in New York and aid was immediately granted. The Kobe community rented houses, arranged them for group living and settled an ever-increasing number of refugees as comfortably as possible. Mrs. S. remembered people sleeping Japanese style, on tatami floors, covered with colorful futons, so much like the *perinehs* (down comforters) given to Jewish brides in their dowries in Europe. Everyone received a daily cash allowance; medical care was arranged through Japanese physicians who often did not charge for their help. Even some very special needs of strictly observant Orthodox Jews received close attention.

A Japanese Christian minister, Dr. Kotsuji, I learned later, was enlisted to negotiate an extension of the brief period during which transit visas for the growing number of European Jews could be valid. Without his enormous skill in maneuvering and his connections in the Japanese government, which was by then clearly afraid of offending the Nazis, the story of the Jews in Kobe might have been different. Many people in Kobe, not just the Jewish community, cooperated on their behalf as long as it was humanly possible.

When Japan declared war on the United States, conditions changed radically. The authorities decided to deport all the refugees from Europe to China. Despite repeated efforts to delay the deportation from Kobe, Mrs. S., her husband and son were shipped—the word she used—to Shanghai.

When Mrs. S., her husband and small boy arrived in Shanghai, they found the city teeming with thousands of other Jewish refugees from Europe. Housing was practically nonexistent, with the tiniest space hard to come by. Work was scarce, no matter what one's training or profession.

After the beauty and what she called the "heavenly" climate of Kobe, Shanghai was a nightmare. Hot in summer and generally miserable for the rest of the year, it was a place Mrs. S. did not care to discuss in detail. No more than she would describe the trip on the boat from Vladivostok to Japan. From her expression, which normally sparkled, I could tell that the years in Shanghai were a torment to her and to her family, but as to many of us who did not go through the Nazi concentration camps, nothing to moan over. It was a difficult period; but they got along somehow or other.

After all, housing was provided, even if there were two hundred souls to a room. Schools were available, some even having Jewish names. The Japanese, in the final analysis, rejected the Nazi plan for exterminating Jews. Even synagogues were permitted to exist in Shanghai!

I gathered from what Mrs. S. did not say, as much as from her words, that any complaints would be unseemly. Others recall their war years in Shanghai with bitterness and pain.

When the war was over, whoever could do so left China for other parts of the world. Mrs. S., her husband and son emigrated to the United States and finally settled in New York. Their son, a teenager by then, studied in public schools and did well, as always, in his schooling.

When Mrs. S. was forty-five years old, her husband died after a prolonged and costly illness. She was left without means. He had not received his license to practice medicine in America before he died. She had no money and no profession and she had to support herself and help see her son through college. She enrolled in a course to learn the practice of radiology as a laboratory technician. After graduation she administered cobalt treatments for some seventeen years in a New York City hospital.

She remarried. I asked about her second husband. She almost giggled in her crystal-like, tinkling voice and assured me he was exceedingly handsome. A regular Don Juan! She took his picture from a table where a huge collection of ornately framed photographs surrounded a Tiffany lamp. A tall, striking man, with a thin mustache, gazed at the world knowing he was "a looker." Mrs. S. was married to her second husband for seventeen years by the time they retired from their jobs in New York and moved to Florida.

During her second marriage the most unspeakable tragedy to befall a parent happened to her. Her only child, the brilliant son, whose safety was uppermost in their minds as she and his father left Cracow for Vilna, Vilna for Japan, then China for America, the man who fulfilled his early promise and became a brilliant engineer for a jet propulsion company in California, died of cancer. He left a young wife and a baby son—and his mother.

Mrs. S. told me of her son's death without self-pity. Her young son died, he was the one to be pitied. Her sorrow was reserved for her son's losses, not seeing his own child growing up, not living out his life with his wife, surrounded by their friends, in the midst of satisfying work. The dead are to be pitied. The living go on with their lives. Mrs. S. did not dramatize, she merely recounted.

Her good relationship with her daughter-in-law continues, though the young woman remarried. Mrs. S. speaks of the second husband as special, terrific, with the *r*'s wonderfully rolled once again. One could easily forget that he is not her own flesh and blood. The daughter-in-law and her second husband had a daughter; Mrs. S. treats her as a grandchild equal to her half brother, Mrs. S.'s son's son.

Mrs. S. lost her second husband when she was in her sixties, while living in Florida. They had many friends in the high-rise building overlooking Biscayne Bay. As often happens, without benefit of social clubs, senior citizen centers, organized activities, widows and widowers seek out each others' company in such houses.

One of her neighbors, Mr. S., had lost his wife soon after she had lost her second husband. What's more, this man's life paralleled her own tragedy. His only son died two days before his wife did. He was left quite alone, as was she. And so they married, she for the third time, he the second.

Mrs. S. told me that her third husband's son was a violinist many years ago. He graduated from the Curtis Institute in Philadelphia, my husband's alma mater. It turned out later that a friend of Walter's and this man's son were good friends in their student days, and played in the same symphony orchestra. "It's a small world" is not a cliché; it is truth. A Greek friend says, "The world is made up of seven people and they all know each other."

Mrs. S. continued with the story. Mr. S.'s son was pushed from early childhood, by his mother and grandfather, to study the violin. In his late twenties, after years of practice, study and playing, he decided against remaining a violinist and entered medical school. All his medical training and expertise, however, could not save him from a long and painful struggle with cancer.

After Mrs. S. told me about her third husband's son, she turned her full attention to telling me Mr. S.'s own life story. It poured out easily, without hesitation, as if she'd gone over all the details many times in her mind.

In his youth, Mr. S. was a struggling insurance agent in Philadelphia. He lived with his wife and son in the same house as his in-laws. Mr. S. and his father-in-law "had words" early on in his first marriage, and for twenty years they shared a home without once speaking to one another. "Can you imagine living like that?" Mrs. S. wanted to know. She could not. The father-in-law pushed his daughter, Mr. S.'s wife, into giving piano lessons, since he deemed it was necessary that yet another income help support the household. The father-in-law was a conductor, without steady employment, so perhaps it was necessary, she added.

After many years of this difficult existence Mr. S. was able to move out of his in-laws' home and live with his wife and son in their own apartment. His business improved. Life became more pleasant, though his wife's health was precarious throughout their marriage.

Mrs. S. grew silent. Suddenly she turned, full-face, to me, took off her glasses and asked with great intensity: "Who was the man you think I loved most, who was the best of my three husbands?" I was stunned by the question. No one in my family would have posed it, or maybe I was only thinking of Mama. The importance Mrs. S. seemed to attach to my answer made me uneasy. I remained silent for a few moments.

Had she given me enough time to collect my thoughts, I would have said that her first husband, the husband of her youth, the father of her child, would have been the one she loved most.

I would have been dead wrong. The man she loved most, she said, the husband who gave her nine of the happiest years of her entire life, was Mr. S., who was eighty and she sixty-six when they got married. Mrs. S. seemed like a young girl, in the first throes of love, when she described his virtues: his kindness, his good looks, his abhorrence of unkind words and deeds against others. He did not tolerate gossip, he would not allow slander.

One evening, Mrs. S. told me, after placing the glasses back on her face, he came to call on her and stayed way past the usual hour for such neighborly visits. She wondered out loud when he planned to go to his own apartment, three flights below hers, identical in layout and size to the one she and her second husband occupied. After all, Mrs. S. girlishly said to him, it was getting very late.

Mr. S. replied that he was not going back to his own apartment. He would stay with her, he said. Mrs. S. looked hesitantly at me, as if I were the older woman and she a young girl, as if I would not approve of her moral standards. And he did stay with her, she continued, until they got married a short time later, and she moved to his apartment three stories below.

Some months after their wedding, she helped him fulfill his wish of returning to Russia, which he left while still a boy, of meeting relatives he hadn't seen in years, of walking the streets and parks of his childhood. It was, she dreamily said, their honeymoon, a strange word to use for people their age—didn't I think—but a honeymoon nonetheless.

Mr. and Mrs. S. went on a group tour, they laughed, they drank, they enjoyed each moment immensely. Hearing her story was like breathing clean air, like drinking fresh water, like hearing the Tchaikovsky Serenade for Strings. Her apartment, in which I heard this story, is filled with antiques and Oriental rugs, and furniture from another era. It is like a stage set for a Chekhov or Turgenev play, except the characters in it had been, and one still is, happy despite tragedy and losses that would trample the spirits of lesser mortals. All the stories she told me while I perched on the edge of an ornately carved chair, seemed to unfold like a drama, not like the life of an "ordinary," gray-haired lady in southern Florida.

After nine blissful years, Mr. S. died. Mrs. S. recounted it as is her wont, without self-pity. She is a woman who has seen much, suffered greatly, made peace with her lot. When she went to the Social Security office to arrange for official documents after Mr. S.'s death, the clerk asked her somewhat incredulously, "How many husbands did you have?" "Three," she told him, "and they all died of natural causes." Laughing as she related it to me, she also laughed when she informed the clerk that she had not fed mushroom soup to any one of her husbands.

Mrs. S. goes on with her life. She takes part in every community activity offered nearby. In addition to singing in her choir, she goes to current-events lectures, to old movies in the social hall, to meetings of Hadassah, ORT, Magen David, and other charitable organizations in which she feels she can be helpful. She attends synagogue services. She goes to concerts. She keeps up with new movies and theater when it comes to Miami Beach. She reads voraciously and watches television programs that interest her. She leads a fuller life than people half her age, with the enthusiasm of a budding long-distance runner, practicing for a world record.

As I was saying good-bye to Mrs. S. we hugged each other warmly and I told her that she is a remarkable, admirable woman. "Am I really?" she asked brightly. "Do you really think so?"

Dovid and Rivkah

In early springtime, during our 1988 visits to Israel, we went to Safed. After Jerusalem, and Vilna, it is the most beautiful place on earth—to me. High in the hills of Galilee, quiet, filled with small, ancient synagogues and many old, and new, artists' galleries, it gives me peace. Safed does not appear in the Old Testament, but Jews have lived there for as long as there have been Jews in the land of Canaan.

Although we had visited Safed twice before, we didn't remain there for more than a few hours. Few tourists linger after seeing the old houses of prayer and the new ateliers of painters, sculptors and artisans along the winding, small streets on top of Mount Canaan. In March 1988 we stayed two days, and those were too brief for all that happened.

After visiting synagogues that were open, and several artists' studios, including one of an ultra-Orthodox French-born painter, who was on a ladder painting his house in anticipation of Passover, we went to the communal art center in the middle of town. As we were its only visitors, we looked undisturbed and unbothered by jostling tourists, who'd stop in Safed for an hour, on their way to Tiberias. To us it was a mixed blessing. In 1988 tourism was not one of Israel's great money producers. I was glad for the peace and quiet in the art center, sad for the reason that caused it.

The elderly couple, who seemed in charge, left us alone. When we found nothing of particular interest, I asked the couple whether there were artists from Vilna in Safed. Something about Safed has always reminded me of "home," which Vilna always will be, no matter where I live or visit. "Yes," both said, almost in unison.

"His name is Dovid Labkovsky. A real aristocrat," the woman said.

"His wife, Rivkah, too," the man added. "A real lady! She was a teacher in Vilna." I liked it that artist and aristocrat, teacher and lady were synonymous in their minds, as they are in mine.

The couple told us that Dovid and Rivkah were old, in frail health. They pulled out a dusty, well-thumbed portfolio from a large bin and showed us drawings and prints by Labkovsky. They told us that the artist and his wife lived in the artists' colony close to the beautiful Moorish-style inn where we were staying.

When we got back to the inn at dusk, it was almost entirely empty. We ate very early and went back to our room to telephone the Labkovskys.

As I was about to dial the Labkovskys' number, I had second thoughts. What if they felt invaded? What right did I have to call them just because we shared a city in our past? Walter urged me on. He knew that anyone from Vilna would find a warm welcome in our house and since we were all made in the same mold, he expected the Labkovskys to feel likewise.

After several false starts, I finally dialed the complete number. A woman's old but assertive voice answered. I spoke in Yiddish and introduced myself as a native of Vilna. Was this Mrs. Labkovsky, and could we come by, possibly buy a piece of her husband's art? Rivkah Labkovsky immediately turned skittish, almost abrasive. There were no pictures of Vilna for sale. She seemed uninterested in our visit. When I apologized and said we wouldn't come, we didn't wish to impose, she immediately set a time for the following morning, gave us her address and hung up.

Once made, the appointment had to be honored. As Walter and I turned into a tiny lane in the artists' colony, a very old man, who carried two plastic bags in one hand and leaned on a cane with the other, came toward us. Walter asked in Hebrew if he might know where the artist Labkovsky lived. The frail man identified himself as Dovid Labkovsky, but he refused to let us help him carry his bags.

He looked exhausted not only by his walk, but by life. He motioned for us to follow him up a short but steep flight of rickety stairs. We entered a tiny, disheveled kitchen. A table, three old chairs, a two-burner gas stove and a few half-open cabinets took up all the space. The artist sat down, flung his shopping bags to the table, but did not take off his jacket, cap or scarf. His face was covered with drops of perspiration. Standing uneasily near him, we waited until the artist had caught his breath and regained strength.

After a while he asked in Hebrew why we had come. I replied in Yiddish that we'd spoken to his wife, and that she approved of our coming. We wanted to buy a picture by an artist from Vilna. I stumbled over my words, trying to tell him as quickly as possible how being from Vilna has shaped my life. His wife had said that he had no paintings of Vilna for sale, but that was all right. I really liked drawings or sketches as much as paintings—sometimes better.

Dovid's face softened when I spoke of Vilna. Walter looked at me, with a gleam that clearly indicated "I told you!" Well, Dovid said, he'd see what he had and asked us to follow him into the next room. He shuffled in his old brown shoes with untied laces, which spun scenarios of falls and cracked ribs through my head. But he reached his small daybed safely and sat down on the edge. Near it were tall shelves with large artist's portfolios divided into many compartments.

There was no sign of Rivkah Labkovsky, and I dared not ask for her. Emboldened, however, by being invited into his room, not just into the kitchen, I told Dovid about my school in Vilna, and the teacher who taught art there from first grade on. Her name was Regina Weinreich. I thought he might know her, her husband, Dr. Max Weinreich, and her father, Dr. Cemach Shabad, who were among the founders of YIVO. Dovid was attentive and asked for the name of my school. When I told him, his face lit up. "I knew the founder, and director, Sofia Markovna Gurewicz, when we were young." He also knew the Weinreichs and Dr. Shabad in Vilna. Once started on the subject, neither of us could stop.

Suddenly, from behind a tall cabinet a woman appeared. She leaned on a walking stick, but stretched out a hand and introduced herself. Rivkah Labkovsky. Small, stooped, with short, curly, salt-and-pepper hair, she had arthritic but still lovely hands. I first look at hands when I meet someone new. Then I look at eyes. Rivkah Labkovsky's were inquisitive, darting in every direction, like a quick-shutter camera photographing scenes from a moving train. A stern, strong presence.

At first I found speaking with Rivkah Labkovsky extremely awkward, even unnerving. As we discovered common references to Vilna, people we knew, similar war memories, the ice was broken. Walter, used to such conversations when people from Vilna discover each other, stood by patiently and smiled.

At last, with effort but refusal of help, Dovid took out several portfolios from the cabinets. The first sketch, in the first portfolio, showed a very old man who sat on a crate, his hands resting on a cane, looking at us questioningly as if he, too, was in the room. I told the artist immediately, without waiting to see other drawings, that I loved it. He quickly informed me that this sketch was not for sale. He continued to turn pages in his first portfolio, then in the second, and then in the third. Many of the sketches and drawings were beautiful. Men and women, and scenes of Safed, were spread before us on the artist's daybed and small table. One sketch of a young girl's and an old woman's heads, looking alike, was especially lovely. None, however, had the power of the old man with the piercing gaze who sat on a crate and held on to his cane.

Though nearly thirty-eight years of marriage has provided us with an unspoken language, and Walter knew how I felt about the sketches in the portfolios, he said that he liked the one with the two female heads very much indeed. He did it, in his thoughtful way, to please the artist, but my nod was only halfhearted and I said nothing.

Rivkah, who stood by silently while we looked at the portfolios, suddenly said that if we'd like to see Dovid's oil paintings, she'd take us to his studio. I could hardly believe that a studio existed in the neglected small apartment. Before leading us out of the gloomy room where we looked at the sketches, she pointed to the wall near the cabinet behind which she had hidden. A gleaming painting with a cascade of flowers hung on it. It was the last picture Dovid had painted: a surprise for her birthday one year ago. He could no longer hold brushes in his aching arthritic fingers.

When Rivkah opened the door to the adjoining chamber, Walter and I were stunned by the incredibly large and airy space, filled with bright sunlight streaming from windows that looked over the hills of Safed. Dazzling paintings stood against walls, hung all around us, were propped up on chairs. Scenes from Vilna, striking portraits of people in markets, in old synagogue yards in my city, in the ghetto, in Ponar during World War II. Powerful pictures of prisoners in the Gulag, where Dovid spent nearly six years, as well as vibrant paintings of Sholem Aleichem and his world, klezmer musicians of long ago—a vanished world, come to life in brilliant color, tucked away in a studio high in the hills of Safed, seen at that time by few, appreciated by almost no one.

Our joy in the paintings pleased Rivkah. "We've been waiting for people like you for years." Then she added quietly, "I think you'll bring us luck." Her words did not surprise me, nor make me feel special. Belief in luck can be self-fulfilling. I've seen it happen before. In the end, however, it would be the pictures that would bring luck to the old couple.

Months after our visit, in one of the letters we'd gotten from Rivkah, we learned that the tide of neglect of Dovid Labkovsky's work had turned. A permanent collection of his work, in a specially designed gallery, had been established in the beautiful town of Ramat Gan, a short ride away from Tel Aviv. Rivkah wrote in her elegant, if sometimes archaic English, that she and Dovid were asked to the opening, that they sat in chairs that looked like thrones, and received people as if they were king and queen. "The mayor of Ramat Gan was there, representatives of the government, people from the radio and even television!" And so Rivkah was right. Their luck turned as she had predicted during our springtime visit in the year 1988.

Rivkah's conversation, and comments on the paintings, alternated between Yiddish, Russian and Polish with me, and Hebrew, German and English with Walter, with many variations in between. She had been a teacher of German and Latin in her youth in Vilna; graduated from the Tarbut, a Hebrew gymnasium, later the university and teacher's institutes. During Dovid's incarceration in the Gulag, she followed him to Siberia and taught in a teacher's institute there—also Latin, German and English. She quoted long passages of the poet Heinrich Heine to Walter, without a pause, in impeccable German.

We spoke of artists in Safed whose work we saw the previous day. I asked her opinion of the man who painted his house, to me his least complicated canvas. They were interesting, she said, but "without life." They were creating geometry, mathematics; those artists' pictures did not tell stories on canvas. Her husband's paintings were not in vogue; they told tales of times and people, of a culture gone by. Not dots and lines and squares and triangles. Paintings, she firmly told us, are shadows of life—and reproductions, she continued, were shadows of shadows. Why did we not consider buying a painting?

The night before, when we spoke on the phone, Rivkah had said they had no paintings of Vilna. Now she was eager for us to buy one! But, to my surprise, my heart was still with the sketches, those quick lines which, like rehearsals not concerts, I love most.

Music suddenly came through the door of the room where we had looked at Dovid's portfolios. It was a symphony by Mahler, one of Walter's favorite composers. He immediately went to join Dovid, who was listening to it on a fine hi-fi system. Although I did not want to part from the paintings and the view from the windows overlooking the hills of Galilee, Rivkah and I also returned to the dark, gloomy room.

Dovid was stretched out on the daybed, eyes tightly shut, listening to the majestic swells of sound. Walter commented on the beautiful tone of the radio. Without opening his eyes, the old artist said that he did not know how he could have survived without it. Their kinship through music, like mine through Vilna, filled Walter with pleasure. He asked whether the hi-fi included a cassette player. It did. He excused himself, whispered that he'd run to the inn and bring a tape of Schubert waltzes he had recorded in New York some years ago. I whispered back that we could mail it, that he should stay, but Walter would not be persuaded.

While I was alone with Rivkah and Dovid we talked in Yiddish, about Vilna's schools, the wonderful libraries and cultural institutions we'd had, about the importance of Vilna's YIVO Institute in Jewish life in New York, of its cooperation with the Jewish Museum in mounting exhibits. I asked if there was something special I could do for them in America. In near unison both said that it was their dream to have a work by Dovid Labkovsky in the permanent collection of the Jewish Museum. Could I see to it when we returned? Could I find out whether a picture that Eleanor Roosevelt had bought from them in the 1950s in Safed was in the archives of the Jewish Museum? She'd promised to donate it, but they had never received a confirmation that it was done. (A thorough search in the museum archives, which I instigated, shows no record of such a donation, nor of any Labkovsky picture in their collection.) Two pictures by Dovid hang in the Yad Vashem Museum in Jerusalem, both of the Vilna ghetto. I saw them; one is a charcoal drawing. Rivkah and Dovid were eager that he be represented in the most prominent Jewish museum in the Diaspora, in New York. I promised to do what I could.

At last Walter returned. Rich, a young American volunteer, came in at about the same time to give of his time, and his strength, to the old couple. Walter gave the cassette to Dovid, who handed it over to Rich to insert in the player. The right buttons were pushed and the clear, bouncy, gay waltz rhythms of Schubert flooded the room. As long as we live, Walter and I shall remember Dovid Labkovsky, rising like a young man from his small daybed, holding his cane with gnarled hands and facing Walter. A radiant smile lit up his sunken, pale face; it transformed him. "Is it really *you* playing this music?" he asked Walter. Walter nodded. The two men stood and looked at each other for a long time. Smiling and listening, listening and smiling.

When conversation resumed, Rivkah asked whether we'd consider buying a painting. Dovid immediately said that he'd *give* us the sketch of the old man. We would never accept it, Walter and I immediately told him. Letting us buy it would be more than enough. How much would it be? "What is it worth?" Dovid turned to Walter for a response. "Two million dollars," Walter said, "but we do not have two million dollars in our account." Still Dovid refused to sell, and name a price. At last, after many entreaties, he relented and named a sum that was honorable for all.

Dovid asked for his special eraser, kept on a shelf in the adjoining studio. While Rich went for it, Dovid took out the sketch of the old man from his portfolio and pointed to a signature in the upper left-hand corner. The man had been a beggar in the marketplace of Safed. When Dovid still walked around town, sketching people from life, he asked the beggar's permission to draw him. When he had finished, Dovid signed the sketch and showed it to his subject.

The old beggar insisted on signing his name, too, in the upper left-hand corner, directly above Dovid Labkovsky's. He even used the artist's crayon. The old man said that since Dovid drew him, his name as well as the artist's belonged on the picture.

Now that Dovid was selling the sketch, he wanted to erase the beggar's name. How many models' names appear on sketches? I prayed that the signature would not totally disappear under Dovid's eraser. My prayer was answered; nothing could make the beggar's name vanish. His strength, like that of the artist, is clearly visible in the picture, in his name as well as his face.

Manon and Roni

She's petite, dark eyed, quicksilver in her motions and speech, very French yet totally Israeli. Her name suits her—she did not change it to a Hebrew name as is often the custom with newcomers to Israel. But her attitude, loyalty and love are deeply rooted in her adopted homeland. She came to Israel at thirteen years of age.

Roni is tall, lean, very quiet, and to hear Manon tell it, very stubborn. A kindred spirit. His conversation is thoughtful and deliberate. He wastes no words. It behooves one to listen carefully when Roni speaks. He was born in Israel and served in its army for four years. Like Manon, he is in his late twenties.

Manon and Roni are married to each other.

She came to Israel with her mother, after her parents' divorce. Her mother is a biochemist, professor at Hebrew

University in Jerusalem. At first Manon was miserable in her new land. She did not know Hebrew, had no friends, missed her life in Paris, her uncles and aunts, grandmother, father, but she adjusted more quickly than others.

Manon's father, a psychiatrist, married twice after his divorce from Manon's mother, both times to Gentile women. Through her father's remarriages, Manon has two Gentile half sisters, and one stepsister too. She likes all three of them, asked them to visit. Over the years not only the girls but their mothers, too, came to Israel to be with Manon.

Manon also has an older brother and sister, both full siblings, children of her mother and father. Each of them is married to a Gentile whom Manon loves. Her brother is a rock musician of international stature. His wife comes from a small island near Mauritius. Their two gorgeous girls have Jewish, Chinese, African and French blood and genes. The whole family has been to Israel. Despite his indifference to Jewish religious observance, Manon's brother feels very Jewish, at home in Jerusalem. He and his family come to visit for short and sporadic periods. But they come.

Her full sister, who is married to a Catholic Frenchman, and Manon are very close, brought even closer by their mother's recent severe illness. The two sisters spent more time together, and with their mother, than they had in years. Their Jewishness is not discussed, nor Israeli life and politics. Their family is their closest bond.

Manon's grandfather, on her father's side of the family, was a well-to-do German Jew. In 1934 he foresaw the tragedies Nazism would cause and moved with his wife to a farm in France. When the war broke out, he was imprisoned as a German; when the Nazis came, they "liberated" him without knowing he was a Jew. His French neighbors never informed the Germans of his background and religion. Others in her family survived the Second World War in France through hiding and serving in the underground.

Manon is a biology teacher in a Jerusalem high school. If looks marked a teacher, she could easily be mistaken for one of her younger students. In the confident and knowledgeable air she exudes when she talks of her profession, she is every inch a leader.

Her enthusiasm for her subject is contagious, even to someone as illiterate in science as I am. Manon becomes a poet when she describes Roni's and her forays into the Negev, or the visits she makes to the desert with her students. Every rock, branch and sign of life on parched earth is a miracle.

Naturally beautiful objects take precedence over value. Their apartment is furnished with very simple natural wood bookcases, wicker and rattan chairs with bright cotton pillows Manon sewed herself. The shelves hold books, driftwood, stones, sculpture, pictures and Manon's handmade pottery, arranged as if they belong only there.

An antique Bedouin kaftan adorns one wall. Before they married, Manon and Roni found it in one of the Arab stalls in the Old City in Jerusalem. In those days it was safe to stroll, look around and shop there. Roni asked Manon whether she'd like to have it instead of a ring. She did and now it hangs like a painting in their apartment. Manon wears it on special occasions.

I'd heard of this kaftan since 1986 when they came to Baltimore, where Roni studied for a master's degree at the Peabody Conservatory with Walter. Although we'd become acquainted during their years in America, it was in Jerusalem during our stays in 1988 that I felt we'd truly met one another. Their friendship and affection are a blessing. I love looking at Manon and being with her. She reminds me so much of my aunt Margola.

After their return to Israel from Baltimore, Roni became a teacher in the Jerusalem conservatory, where he once studied himself. He wrote and published a collection of children's songs for beginning piano students. When he first played it for us, I thought Walter would melt from pure *naches*. Walter's involvement and love for his students is passed on by them to the next generation.

Among Roni's favorite pupils is a talented Arab youngster, who had frequent and long music lessons during Intifada demonstrations in 1988. The boy could not attend regular classes in school and the head of the preparatory division at the conservatory made special arrangements so that he could spend extra time on his piano lessons.

One day, Roni told us, the boy came to his lesson with a song he'd written, both words and music. The song was about how he'd grow up and fight bad men with all his might, kill them with real guns and bullets. He sang it with emotion and fervor, and he accompanied himself enthusiastically on the piano. When he finished, Roni asked him which bad men he planned to kill with real guns and bullets when he got older. "The Israeli soldiers!" Roni's student replied. "But I am an Israeli soldier, too. Would you want to kill me?" The boy was incredulous at Roni's question.

"You cannot be a bad man, a soldier," the child said. "You are my music teacher! My parents even invited you and your wife to tea! How could this be?" How indeed?

Roni's and Manon's life is not made of easy questions, or easy answers. They are faced daily with history that unfolds before them in Jerusalem, the Golan Heights where Roni served for a long period, in the Gaza Strip, and on the West Bank, where he may have to serve next. In back of them, in shadows that they may try to avoid but cannot, are the histories of their families. Especially those who survived the Holocaust in Europe, as Roni's parents did before coming to Israel in 1946 or 1947.

Roni's strong-willed mother, a talented painter, and his gentle father, supervisor of curriculum for elementary schoolchildren in Jerusalem and the author of texts used in Israeli schools, met after the war. She was born in Czechoslovakia and he in Poland. They survived ghettos and camps, married, worked hard and raised two sons. After thirty years together, they got a divorce; each now lives alone. Roni's father seems at peace with his world. His mother rails against the people in her neighborhood and building; they are ultra-Orthodox in their religious observance, disapprove of her work at the easel on Sabbath and holidays, make their opinions exceedingly clear.

Manon and Roni also lead secular lives. Once Roni remarked, while driving with us on Sabbath eve, which defies the commandment of rest on the seventh day of the week, that he missed Jerusalem Sabbaths the most when they were in Baltimore. Though he was at the wheel of his car, and we were with him, his words were not incongruous to Walter or me. He was sharing his deep feeling for his city, for the custom, for being a Jew, though not for the religious observance of some of his countrymen.

However, Roni and Manon helped me find the way to an experience that more observant friends considered foolhardy, even dangerous.

It took place on the last day of Succoth, the holiday that celebrates the fall harvest and commemorates the days after the exodus from Egypt, when Jews wandered in the wilderness and lived in huts. The last day of Succoth is called Simchath Torah, the day of rejoicing in the Torah, when the last chapter of the Five Books of Moses, and we once again begin the first chapter to indicate that the study of Torah never ends. The beginning of Simchath Torah is celebrated in Israel on the eve of the sixth day of Succoth. All over the Diaspora, it starts in the evening of the seventh day, since Succoth is celebrated for eight days throughout the world, but in Israel for seven days only.

We arrived in Jerusalem in the fall of 1988 in the afternoon, a few hours before that evening's celebration of Simchath Torah was to be held all over the city. We went to the Western Wall, expecting huge crowds dancing with Torahs, as we had seen in photographs in years gone by. Instead, we found a small and subdued group of celebrants, not more than twenty or thirty men and boys holding up the Torah on the men's side of the wall. Intifada kept away the tourists, and the local population of Jerusalem celebrated this joyous and noisy Jewish holiday in their own synagogues.

Although we went to a formal service the next day in the largest and most beautiful synagogue in Jerusalem, I felt a sense of loss, of not having seen or participated in an often dreamed of, vividly imagined, Simchath Torah celebration in the Holy Land.

I had heard from friends and relatives in New York that many small, very Orthodox synagogues in Mea She'arim where Hassidic Jews live and pray, also observe Simchath Torah on the same day as it is celebrated in the Diaspora. None of Walter's friends in Jerusalem believed that this custom was still observed; they assured us that the holiday truly ended after sundown of the seventh day, but I would not give up my quest.

Walter agreed to attend a concert with Alik and Bracha at the Targ Center in Ein Kerem, an invitation I turned down. I could hear string quartets all over the world; to be part of a Simchath Torah observance in Mea She'arim in Jerusalem might happen to me only once in my lifetime.

Everyone but Roni and Manon was appalled that I planned to go alone to a deeply Orthodox community, at night. People would consider me odd. I'd be uncomfortable, maybe treated rudely. There were recent acts of violence in the district. Broken glass was found in challah bread purchased for the holiday. None of this deterred me. Besides, Roni had heard of celebrations in Mea She'arim.

Spurred on by Manon's and Roni's smiling approval I dressed in perfectly acceptable Hassidic fashion: a dark, high-necked, long-sleeved dress, plain stockings, a silk scarf wound around my head in the manner of Orthodox women. I wear such a "hat" even in New York; it keeps my hair neat and I find it comfortable. Certainly it would make me inconspicuous in the world of Mea She'arim. Manon and

Roni drove me there after nightfall, when cars were permitted. They pointed the way to various streets on which small synagogues were located, and they gave me directions to find a bus back to the hotel. They wished me luck and drove away.

On my own, I approached two women on a Mea She'arim street, one young, pushing a baby carriage with two slightly older children holding on to her skirt, and the other toothless, and probably quite old. I spoke in Yiddish, told them I was from Vilna, which broke the ice, and asked for help in finding a *shul* in which Simchath Torah might be observed on this night. They smiled. No, services would not be held, the old woman said. "This is not the Jerusalem of Lithuania, this is Jerusalem!"

Undaunted, I walked up and down little dark streets, listening for sounds of Simchath Torah dancing and music. After all, Manon and Roni thought I'd find it. A small nuts and dried fruit stand was open, but when I asked for directions in Yiddish I found that the proprietor was Moroccan and spoke only Hebrew. I brought a bag of peanuts and continued my quest.

At last, facing defeat, I followed Manon's instructions, found the bus that would take me back to our hotel and got on. After one or two stops, I noticed a platform being set up in a small square, with music stands and all manner of signs in Hebrew. Sensing an impending gathering and hoping it might be a public Torah celebration such as those held in Crown Heights and Borough Park in Brooklyn, I got off the bus and walked back to the square.

A few men with long black coats, large hats and long,

119

flowing beards, were setting up the stands. Still fewer on-lookers, similarly dressed, hovered nearby. I was afraid to ask any one of them a question, for fear that a strange woman's queries might not be welcome. I decided to hover, too, without saying a word, waiting to see what might happen later.

More people gathered, several women among them. I asked one of them, in Yiddish, whether she knew what was afoot. She understood my question, but answered in very proper, British-accented English that Agudath Israel, a political party, was about to conduct a rally. There were sure to be many speeches, and music, too.

I'd never been to a political rally in Israel, let alone one in which the candidates wore fur *shtraimels,* those incredible Hassidic hats, and long black coats. Maybe they would even campaign in Yiddish? I had been "brought up," even in adulthood, by the dictum of Ha'rav Joseph Soloveitchik who said that rabbis should not become politicians. Politics and religion did not make good partners. He said so, in different words, when he was offered by David Ben Gurion, more than once, the position of chief rabbi of the State of Israel. Manon and Roni agree with the view of Dr. Soloveitchik, but they would enjoy hearing what I thought of the rally. And I was in Mea She'arim because of their encouragement.

Musicians tested the sound system; sweet klezmer clarinet playing came over the microphone, then a fiddle, then drums. I knew it would be a long night. I was hooked, and I went to find a place to sit or at least perch. A ledge across the square was the only possibility, so I quickly ran to it and sat down without looking back. When I did, I realized that on the other side the ledge dropped at least twenty feet into a courtyard strewn with garbage. I'd create quite a scene if I fell into the refuse. I clutched the ledge with all of my strength.

People streamed toward the square in all directions, as if the klezmer sounds were a magnet. Police cars cordoned off the streets and all buses and private cars were diverted. People surrounded me on all sides. A woman, with gaunt cheeks and a battered face, stood right in front of me. She had dyed red hair, no scarf covered her head, nor did she wear a wig like Orthodox women. Totally unkempt, with a furious look in her eyes, she snarled angrily at a little boy by her side. He did not wear a skullcap, I saw, nor did he have sidelocks in the manner of Hassidic boys. His small face was contorted with fear and anguish. He kept embracing the woman's legs; she shook him off like a pesty animal. Suddenly I realized that the woman had no arms or hands, that only flipperlike appendages came out directly from her elbows. She wore sandals without stockings. Her blouse had a deep V-neckline and was smudged and soiled in many places.

Women, dressed in Hassidic holiday garb, passed by and nodded to this woman, without uttering a word. They obviously knew her. She must have lived in their community— but she might as well have come from the moon. When the little boy continued to irritate her, she gave him a shove with one knee and walked away. With a sharp cry he ran after her until they were swallowed up by the ever-growing crowd. The mystery of who she was, how she fit in the life of Mea She'arim, who battered her face, who fathered her son, haunts me. I worry for the little boy too.

Next to me on the ledge, a young, blond woman observed

everything as keenly as I did. She was a British nurse, who stopped in Israel for a one-week holiday and stayed an entire year, working in a hospital in one of the country's smaller cities. She came to Jerusalem, and particularly to Mea She'arim, she said, for "your holiday with the Torah." When I explained to her that the platform being set up was not for a religious celebration but for a political rally she seemed truly disappointed. In Great Britain, she said, "the holiday with the Torah" was celebrated on the eighth day of "the holiday when you eat outside of your houses, in sort of a lean-to, in the yard." She seemed to know quite a bit about Succoth. Much more than I knew about the political speeches that had begun to ring out throughout the square. Everything was said in Hebrew, and the only words I understood were *Likud, God, Shamir* and *shalom,* and a few other scattered sentences referring to the political situation in Israel in the fall of 1988.

In between the speeches the klezmer band played familiar melodies. Bearded jugglers with skullcaps and black coats came up to the platform and performed incredible tricks with bottles that they balanced on their foreheads, noses and chins. They threw balls in every direction, up in the air, down to the floor, sideways; four, five, six, seven balls were flying around like big yellow birds. The crowd was enthralled.

After the tenth or fifteenth, or twentieth speech, I decided to make my way back to the hotel. Taking a bus, according to Roni and Manon's careful instructions, was not possible. Since streets were cordoned off and all bus routes and traffic diverted, I could have become totally lost while looking for the right bus. Walking back to the hotel seemed simpler, but trying to recall every one of Manon's backup directions, "take this left, then this right, then another left," if I did decide to walk, was not easy either.

As I was wending my way through one small dark street after another, I suddenly heard singing, clapping and stomping. I walked in the direction from which the sound came— along a small path, through stones and rubble in an unkempt courtyard, until I finally came upon a synagogue in which every window was open, and which pulsated with a life all its own.

Women of all ages, dressed very much as I was—three, four, five, six deep—clung to each other and pressed their faces to the outside bars on every window of the synagogue. I stood in the back of the crowd near one of the windows. After a while, I was pushed to the front, pressed my face to the iron gate and peered eagerly at the scene in the room.

Swarms of men of all ages danced with Torahs, each forming a separate circle. Their heads were thrown back, faces ecstatic, their hands raised high—snapping, clapping, waving kerchiefs, holding the Torahs. An old man and a young boy stood to one side. The long-bearded sage played a clarinetlike instrument that I'd not seen before. The tremulous voice of the child wailed, cried and rejoiced. None of the strange, soulful songs sounded familiar. They probably came from Spain or Africa, or another source of Sephardic tradition.

Bodies moved as one to the melodies. It all seemed dreamlike. I would have stayed there all night had not many other women's bodies pressed against mine to look inside, to participate in their own way in the celebration.

At last I knew I had to go back to the hotel, to call Roni

and Manon, to tell them what I'd heard and seen. But I did not call them that night. Since Walter was late returning from the concert, I sat alone in the room overlooking the Old City. My hunger to partake of Jerusalem's spirit and rituals was well satisfied; speaking of it might have broken the spell.

Roni and Manon invited us to dinner later that week, on our last Sabbath eve in Jerusalem in October. Roni, as always, prepared a wonderful combination of hot, Oriental foods and fresh salads, all vegetarian, all delicious, all healthy. We talked about the upcoming elections. Roni is opposed to the Likud party line. He wants peace, not at all cost, but a just and lasting peace for all. He'd lost too many friends, fought too many battles. Enough! Enough wars! He would have fumed at the political rally in Mea She'arim, the one I attended thanks to him and Manon.

We talked about the baby they were expecting in December. Our Israeli "grandchild." Manon pulled out her family photo albums yet another time for me to pore over, to sort out her complicated, marvelous, multifaceted family. Roni played for Walter in another room. His music, their home, the atmosphere of Sabbath filled me with peace. I couldn't bear the thought that our visit was ending.

As we were about to leave, I told Roni and Manon that we planned to go again to the Western Wall in the morning, on our last day in Jerusalem. I wanted to put new *kvittels* in the wall, to send messages to the Almighty and pray for good health, and peace, for all of us. "I hope there'll be enough room in the cracks." I've always been afraid of dislodging other supplicants' papers.

Roni looked at me in his thoughtful way and assured me that all *kvittels* that fall out of the Kottel's stones are collected. "What's done with them?" I asked fearfully. I'd never asked anyone this question before, lest the answer shatter my childish illusion of sending a direct written message to God.

"Why," Roni quietly told me, "they are carefully gathered and buried in holy ground by the Hassidic caretakers at the Wall."

A miraculous sense of relief swept over me and made me weep with total abandon. Roni's respectful tone, the voice of this secular, tough Israeli soldier, this rationalist, pragmatist, reached the depths of my soul. I dared not look directly at him, nor at Walter, and barely at Manon, who had tears in her eyes as I whispered words they could barely hear.

To lighten the mood, Roni suddenly asked, "What is it you're writing?"

"A book," I replied.

"Ah, yes, but what's it about?"

"Different people," I told him.

"Ah, yes, but is there something that links them?"

"Being Jewish," I said.

Barry

I heard this story some time ago. Because the person who told it is a woman of few words—she is a musician and teacher of piano—I trust each one she utters. She told this tale to me in 1988 in Jerusalem, on a clear, moonlit evening at Mishkenot Sha'ananim, the artists' colony that looks over the walls of the Old City. Through the windows we could see the Tower of David, the Armenian church and monastery, and both the Jaffa and the Zion gates. I don't think anyone would dare exaggerate in these surroundings, let alone tell even a small lie. Heaven seemed tuned in to every word.

What's more, a few days before, I noticed the young man of whom she spoke. He sat quite still, looking intently straight ahead. One could sense that all of his being was absorbed in the words and music of the leader of the seminar

126

that we both attended. It was Walter who led the seminar, lectured and played the piano. My observance of my husband's audience, as always, was even more acute than my attention to his words and playing. Those I'd heard before. His audience I was seeing for the first, and probably only, time and my attention was by and large directed at them.

The young man I particularly noticed wore a yarmulke, a head covering worn by all Orthodox male observers of the Jewish faith, but not so common in a music academy, even in Jerusalem. The *tzitzes* (ritual fringes) dangling from beneath a very collegiate-looking, light blue sweater, added to the incongruity of his appearance in the auditorium where we both sat. I liked his eyes, his posture of respectful attention, his utter stillness.

Some years ago this young man, who I will call Barry, was a student of piano at one of the best music schools in New York City. To make ends meet, he played popular and jazz gigs in various clubs and joints in the city. Someone in one of those places introduced him to drugs. Casually at first, but more steadily later on, Barry began to use them. He got hooked. His lessons stopped. I never did learn just how his life fell apart, and guessing at reasons would serve little purpose. But I know families whose children had similar afflictions, so it isn't hard to imagine some details. Barry's family was in turmoil. After many arguments, and soul-searching, they placed him in a drug rehabilitation center.

One day two young men in Orthodox garb came to Barry's room at the center. Who sent them and how they got there I do not know and have not asked. The young men introduced themselves, asked about his welfare. Barry must have told them he was miserable. The withdrawal period was agonizing; he despaired of his future. The young men asked whether he would be willing to trust them with his life; they promised him a cure without drugs and without pain.

Barry, in turn, had to promise that he would leave the center, live in a *yeshivah* in Israel, study Torah for at least five hours each day, become a vegetarian, and observe all the strict dietary and daily laws of an ultra-Orthodox community. He would have to grow a beard and sidelocks, wear *tzitzes*, a long black coat and hat. Barry agreed. His family was appalled, so much so that they threatened to disown him if he pursued this plan. He did anyway.

Barry arrived at the *yeshivah* in Jerusalem. Not only did he have to follow all the instructions told him at the drug rehabilitation center in New York, he also had to drink forty glasses of water a day, on the orders of the *rosh yeshivah*. The head of the *yeshivah* followed the tenets and the religious institutions of long-ago Vilna, and other similar places of learning in a vanished part of Eastern Europe. (His orientation seems to have been that of the Misnagdim, who believed in strict, yet enlightened observance of all Torah teachings, led by the Gaon of Vilna in the 1700s.)

The rabbi was not only learned in religious matters; he must have had some medical training as well. His methods began to cleanse Barry's body of the drugs that had invaded all its cells. Barry studied Torah diligently, as prescribed. He went everywhere with a bottle of water by his side and drank from it to help void the poisons that nearly killed him.

After some months of the regimen, however, Barry got thin and he looked unhappy. The rabbi noticed and asked Barry what troubled him. Barry confessed that he missed the piano. He wanted to play again, to take part in music. He felt that he could not continue to exist without it.

The rabbi did not feel equipped to pass judgment on Barry's abilities in this area. However, he was well acquainted with a wealthy British woman, a music patron in Jerusalem. He telephoned her for advice and said the matter was urgent. She, in turn, telephoned our friend, whom I'll call Mitzpah (which is a rare Israeli name and means both tower and observation point), just as Mitzpah was about to leave to attend a piano recital.

The British music patron insisted that Mitzpah forego the concert to hear Barry that very evening. A compromise was reached. Barry would play for Mitzpah immediately after the recital, in the same hall, which would be made available for this purpose.

Barry arrived at the concert hall for his audition. He seemed to pace even as he sat through the concert, not far from Mitzpah, waiting for his own performance to begin. When it did, at last, he not only had to interrupt his playing to drink his water and to go to the bathroom, but to constantly wipe his hands, which were inordinately damp as well as "rusty" after months without practice. His yarmulke kept sliding off his head. His *tzitzes* dangled to the rhythm of the music. His whole appearance and demeanor left much to be desired, Mitzpah said.

But he played well enough to indicate his potential. Mitzpah was impressed and called the British patron to tell her that Barry was indeed talented and could have a future in music. The patron asked how much it would cost to provide Barry with a private room and piano for one year, so he could work and practice. In her view, the atmosphere, noise, crowds of young men at the *yeshivah* were utterly unconducive to the pursuit of music.

She set conditions to her offer. If Barry accepted, he'd have to live as a musician, devote all his time to practicing and playing, and give up the five hours of Torah study and many of the other obligatory tasks of a *yeshivah* student.

Barry refused without a moment's hesitation. The importance of his promise to study Torah was greater than his hunger for music. He would never give it up. Back and forth "negotiations" were conducted. The patron relented. Barry got a room with a piano near his *yeshivah*; he studied both Torah and music. Yet six months after the patron's offer went into effect, she reneged. There was no musical future, she said, for a young man who did not devote all his time to the pursuit of his muse.

The rabbi gave Barry some assistance. His teacher, Mitzpah, who continued this story, helped, too. Barry received no moral support from other students at the music academy where he was enrolled, let alone any practical aid. But he persisted. Time came around for Barry to play a recital at the academy, part of the examinations given to all music students at the end of the semester. The date of the recital fell in a period when *yeshivah* students may not give time to anything but religious study and observance. Such were the strictures of his *yeshivah* in the Old City in Jerusalem.

Our friend Mitzpah, Barry's teacher, while Jewish and

Israeli-born and bred, was appalled. He would be flunked. A whole semester of work would go down the drain. She telephoned the rabbi. He stood his ground about the importance of the religious observances and hence limitations in secular life imposed during that period. Mitzpah, equally tenacious, explained that Barry's music was art, not idle performing or entertainment. The rabbi promised to reconsider. A disciple of the Gaon of Vilna, though generations later, he relented, gave Barry permission to prepare carefully and then to play his examination recital at the music academy.

When Mitzpah walked into the small recital hall at school, on the day when Barry was to perform, she found a sea of black hats, long coats, men with *tzitzes* at their sides, looking expectantly at the stage. Ladies in *sheitels*, wigs that Orthodox women must wear after they are married, were there as well, sitting to one side, away from all the men, as the laws dictate. One of the women, Mitzpah noticed, sat well in front, with jewels adorning her fingers, earlobes, neck—an older woman of obvious means.

After Barry's performance, the whole audience, his *yeshivah* friends and teachers, gave him a thunderous ovation. It went on and on. As our friend was telling me this story, I felt tears welling in my eyes. Even I. B. Singer could not improve on this tale. But more was to come.

After the concert Barry was besieged backstage by his well-wishers from the Old City. The older lady, with the jewels sparkling all over her ample body, took off a ring from one finger and handed it to Barry. It would bring him luck, overnight, she said when he resisted taking the jewel.

He could return it to her the next day, she said. She lived not far from his *yeshivah*; he'd find her.

Barry, whose naïve nature and goodness were, and still are, well meshed with talent and intelligence, finally did take the ring and put it in his pocket. Our friend, his teacher, Mitzpah, observed it all with amazement and disbelief. But she did not interfere. After the bejeweled woman in the *sheitel* left, Barry asked Mitzpah what he should do next. "Return the ring tomorrow, in the morning, as the woman suggested!" Mitzpah urged Barry to look for her in the Old City, near his *yeshivah,* without delay.

Barry found the woman in the Jewish quarter of the Old City the following morning, without a bit of difficulty. In the Old City it isn't necessary to know a person's full name. A general idea of where the person lives, and a reasonably accurate physical description are almost always enough. In any event, almost everyone is known by his or her first name and occupation only.

Barry returned the ring to the woman who attended his concert, and they chatted politely for a while. She then told Barry, quite ceremoniously, that she had a wonderful *shidach* for him, a perfect match, the finest girl he could meet. A match only made in Heaven. By then Barry seemed to take the rules and cures from Heaven as a matter of daily existence. He did not refuse to meet the girl.

The next thing our friend Mitzpah knew, Barry was engaged. She could not remember how long a time elapsed between the return of the ring and the engagement. A few weeks, several months? Not very long to be making such a major decision in his life.

He told her that the wedding would have to take place
on a date during which final exams in music history, solfeg-
gio and theory were to be given at the academy. Once more
Mitzpah was stunned to learn that the date was set according
to the religious requirements of Barry's rabbi. He might
even forfeit his courses!

She questioned him about the girl. Who was she? How
would they live? He barely eked out a living by doing every
sort of task at the music school, as well as at the *yeshivah*,
in addition to the help he was getting from his rabbi and
from her. His patron's largesse was gone, his parents still
had no contact with him. What would happen?

Well, Barry said, Selena—her real name was even more
romantic, and she hailed from Lancashire in England—was
as committed to Orthodox traditions and teachings as he
was, and she would work. She admired his playing more
than anything in the world, with the exception of their
religion. She wanted to learn to sing herself, had a lovely
voice. They would manage.

Mitzpah asked him whether he loved Selena. He said
yes, and he admired her, and besides, who could say no to
a marriage match arranged by Heaven? The wedding took
place in 1985, not in 1895, when matches "arranged in
Heaven" were more often earthbound. Literally hundreds
of guests descended for the happy event, including Barry's
family from America and Selena's from England.

The dates worked out, too. Barry was even able to take
his exams early and he passed them all. He and Selena live
in the Old City. They have several children now. He continues to study Torah and to play; he earns a living teaching

young children in the preparatory division of the academy where he studied. He plays concerts, he coaches, he does other things. They do manage, very well.

Barry played at my husband's seminar, a wonderful performance of Ravel's *Valses Nobles et Sentimentales*. I heard it before I heard his story. My appreciation of his artistry was purely that of a listener to music, not of an admirer of what he'd done with his life.

Rabbi J. B. Soloveitchik, one of Judaism's greatest scholars, wrote, "... a prime emulation of God is to develop one's unique talents and personality, just as He is one."

If Barry is not the perfect example of the truth of this statement, I don't know who it may be.

Yakov and Chava

The first walk we took on our first Sabbath in Jerusalem when we arrived there in February of 1988 was to the Old City. We put in a *kvittel*—a slip of paper with a request to God, which I wrote in Yiddish to assure an immediate understanding of my message—in the cracks of the Kottel. We begged Him for good health for Paul C., a very ill friend in New York. The Western Wall was filled with *kvittels*. It was difficult to find a crack in which to place ours. A lot of correspondence was being sent to Heaven.

After reciting prayers, putting my cheek against the cool stones of the remnants of the Temple, I suggested to Walter that we look for Yakov, our son's first Hebrew teacher in New York, who lived nearby. This young man had studied at the Jewish Theological Seminary; at that time he was called Jeff and he came from a totally assimilated family on Long Island.

He was an inspiring, wonderful tutor for our son David. I liked the idea of a Hebrew teacher coming to our house. It reminded me of the days in Vilna, where families took *yeshivah* boys into their homes to tutor children, or simply to become part-time members of their households. It helped the boys keep body and soul together, to get a square meal at least once a day. Jeff did not need the meal. Instead he nourished our souls.

The lessons began so inauspiciously, however, that I had wanted to hide in a closet. Permanently. "Do you know the Ten Commandments?" I overheard Jeff asking David on his first visit to our house. "Well, not all of it. My mom never lets me stay up till the end when they play it on TV."

I thought we'd never live this down.

Things improved, and changed. David learned the Ten Commandments, not through Cecil B. De Mille or from the lips of Charlton Heston. He and Jeff studied together, took field trips, talked of many things. As David's lessons with Jeff went on, we noticed that Jeff moved slowly, but inexorably, from the Conservative point of view of Judaism taught at the Jewish Theological Seminary, to the teachings of the Lubavitch Hassidic movement, led by Rabbi Mena-chem Schneerson. At one point, probably before Jeff even graduated from the Seminary, he told David that he did not eat at his parents' home, because it wasn't sufficiently kosher for his beliefs.

"Do you think that's right, Ma?" David asked one after-noon after his lesson was over and Jeff had gone. When at a loss for an answer, I often ask a question instead. "What do you think, David?" I replied. "Well, the Ten Commandments say you have to honor thy mother and thy father. They don't say you have to eat only kosher stuff. It's not fair for him not to eat the food his mom cooks." In our view, David learned his lessons well. Though not necessarily as Jeff thought he taught them.

Jeff graduated from JTS, married Chava, a remarkable young woman from Silver Spring, Maryland, whose religious outlook was moving in the same direction as his. Neither Jeff's nor Chava's parents understood what was happening to their children, and they were not overjoyed when Jeff and Chava moved to the highly structured, some say even restrictive, way of life conducted by the Hassidic Lubavitch community in Crown Heights, Brooklyn. The men wore traditional Hassidic garb, the women shaved their heads and donned *sheitels,* as a sign of modesty. Jeff became involved in Hassidic educational and social-service circles, Chava participated in the life of the community. They felt fulfilled.

David was taught by other young students from the Jewish Theological Seminary. His religious instruction at home continued from age nine until he was sixteen. At his own request in the beginning, with our prodding after his bar mitzvah. Every one of his teachers, from Jeff, his first, to Charles, his last, gave David a different and valuable perspective. They taught him, through Torah and discussion, how to reason and to think. We've kept in touch with each of them, with some frequently, others more rarely.

But Jeff was always special. He became Yakov, moved with Chava and their baby boy, Asher, to Safed, very near Israel's northern border with Lebanon. There he was appointed by the Lubavitch movement as principal of a girls' *yeshivah* high school. The couple and their son lived in the most primitive circumstances. Safed, however, made up for their bleak little place, filled as it is with many ancient synagogues and sitting atop a glorious ridge of hills, overlooking half of Israel, and it seems most of the world. They had another baby, a beautiful, deaf daughter they named Nechama-Leah.

When we came to Jerusalem for our son's bar mitzvah in 1978, Yakov rode on a bus, for nearly five hours, only days after his daughter was born, to be the Bal T'fillah, the leader of the services, at David's coming-of-age ceremony by the Western Wall. This occasion was, for our son, ourselves and all our family and friends, an unforgettable experience. Yakov wore classic Hassidic garb: black coat, large hat, white stockings. David stood next to him, in his classic navy-blue, three-piece bar mitzvah suit, and both of their shining faces are recorded in our memories, and in photographs, for all time. We had purposefully scheduled the bar mitzvah on a Thursday morning, when the Torah is read, so we'd be able to photograph the ceremony, something that would not have been permitted on Sabbath.

In 1981 or 1982 Yakov and his family, which by then included another baby they named Levi, came back to Long Island. Yakov and Chava thought that Nechama-Leah would receive more advanced treatment for her handicap in the United States than in the remote town in the north of Israel. They became part of a small Hassidic community in Suffolk County; we spoke occasionally on the phone, Yakov stopped in to say hello.

Time flew, as it always does, though it seems much faster

as I get older. One Sunday morning the telephone rang. It was Yakov. "I'm here on a visit from Jerusalem! Can I come to see you today?" From Jerusalem? We were certain that Yakov and his brood were still in Long Island. We changed our plans, stayed home to welcome him.

He practically leapt through the door when I opened it. The same young face, with a reddish beard, sparkling dark blue eyes, ebullient manner. Still in Hassidic dress, but not in a long black coat and not wearing a wide-brimmed hat. *Tzitzes* hung beneath his jacket, his frame lanky, tall, intense, full of energy. A radiant young man.

He and Chava had more children, six in all, he said when he visited us on that happy Sunday. The youngest boy had a hearing handicap, the second daughter, born after Levi, had a birth defect, now fully corrected, not discernible at all. The family considered themselves blessed, truly blessed. Whatever fate brought them was God's will and it was accepted. I believed Yakov. His were not trite words, nor spoken with false bravado. He told us how well Nechama-Leah was doing. She learned Sign language both in English and Hebrew, read lips perfectly, had a happy, sunny disposition. "Just like you!" I said. He laughed.

"I'm director of a Hassidic outreach program in the Old City, working mainly with young people from America, Australia, England, Canada." He was on the edge of his chair as he described the work he was doing and the response it brought from men and women in their teens and twenties. Most of them were, like Yakov (in his previous existence as Jeff), from assimilated families and without much background in religious observance.

Who supported his work, we asked. The Lubavitch

movement in New York? "The Lubavitch community gave us financial support the first year of our service. Now we are on our own," Yakov answered. The students themselves, their families, their friends, a huge network of people helped him in his work. He had to become a fund-raiser as well as a teacher. He was very good at it. It was impossible not to be swept along by Yakov's enthusiasm.

And so we were in Jerusalem, exactly ten years after our son's bar mitzvah. It was also a milestone for Walter. He first walked the streets of this golden city nearly fifty years earlier, when he escaped the Nazis in Vienna, to study at the Jerusalem Conservatory. A half century earlier it was not possible to visit the Kottel, the Wailing Wall as it was called then. Arabs shot randomly at any Jew who attempted such a mission.

The Chabad House, to which we had addressed letters for Yakov and Chava, was closed. It was past midday. We asked for directions to his home. Everyone near Chabad House knew him, but directions to his place were so complicated that we got lost not once, but twice. Finally a young man, who would only identify himself as Fat Phil (almost everyone we met in the Old City was known by a first name, or nickname), took us practically by our hands and led us to Yakov's doorstep.

Yakov's oldest son, Asher, a serious boy of twelve or so, wearing aviator glasses, looked at us suspiciously. That we were not family friends, or Hassidim, was obvious, and that we were much too old to be his father's students was equally clear. Nevertheless, Asher opened the door to his house and let us in. After an initial look of total mystification and shock on her face, Chava welcomed us as if we were the Messiah's *shelichim*, or messengers of good tidings. (In her *sheitel* and scarf, Chava seemed a typical Hassidic housewife, but stereotyping is very deceiving. A former English major, she tries to keep a journal; a talented potter, she goes to class once a week where, I later learned to my joy and astonishment, she has met and become friends with Manon. Despite their totally opposite life-styles, and religious observances, Manon and Chava had found much in common.)

Chava took us to an enormous room that was filled to the edges by a long table and several dozen chairs squeezed close together. Young men and women, and a few older people on the side, filled every inch of space, books in hand, faces serious and intent. Obviously a discussion had been in progress. Yakov looked up, jumped as if he'd gotten an electric jolt, embraced Walter. I could not even shake his hand; the strict rules of Hassidic observance do not permit any bodily contact between men and women not related to one another. It did not really matter. His beaming face, and welcoming words and gestures, more than made up for lack of bodily contact. All his children surrounded us. The littlest one, who did not hear well, made baby-talk noises in Hebrew. The daughter who'd had a speech problem due to a birth defect chattered like a hummingbird in Hebrew and English. Every word was as clear as a bell. The four-year-old girl and ten-year-old son, Levi, and Asher, were all parents could wish for, too. Nechama-Leah beamed at us. She *is* sunny and beautiful. Chava translated for her in Sign language what we were saying.

Several weeks later we heard this deaf child intone the

Four Questions at their Seder, the first one Walter and I spent in Jerusalem together, and the first one we'd ever celebrated with a Hassidic family. The unusual sounds coming from her lips, the look on her face, the looks on the faces of her brothers and sisters as they silently moved their own lips to Nechama-Leah's prayer, stay in the heart. The fifth question might have been, "How did she do it?" and their answer surely would be, "By the power of prayer and love." They were a truly blessed family, just as Yakov had told us in New York.

We also felt blessed by being with them on our first Sabbath in Jerusalem in over a decade. A place of honor was made for Walter at the head of the table. He looked somewhat uneasy, but pleased at the fuss. I could imagine the thoughts going through his head. "Suppose they ask me to read some portion of the prayerbook? Suppose I don't do it perfectly?" Yakov didn't. Walter seemed relieved.

Instead Yakov turned to me, seated at the other end of the long table, among his numerous female students, with one of his little girls cuddled on my lap, hugging, kissing, embracing me as if I were a cherished relative. My knees grew weak; my Hebrew was nonexistent and my religious education very shaky indeed. Not a particle of my brain felt ready to participate in the serious study of Judaism that was obviously taking place around Yakov and Chava's table.

"Esther, tell us one of your *meises*, a good story," he said. My head began to spin, and not from jet lag. Which story, which *meise* would the people at this table be interested in hearing? We did not come to tell stories; we came to wish Yakov and his family a good Shabbes.

Yakov kept urging me, the others at the table looked expectantly in my direction. Yakov said that I was a writer. What could I do? Refuse my son's first Hebrew teacher, the one who'd heard that David did not know all of the Ten Commandments because I packed him off to bed before the end of the film?

I told them one story, they wanted another. "Tell us about you and your mother and the storm in Siberia," Yakov urged. He'd read my book some years before. I looked over at Walter; he nodded vigorously in support of Yakov's request. There was nothing to do but tell of the time I was lost in a storm.

"While we were in exile, I knitted, embroidered and crocheted for women who paid me in various goods and also with money. Once I took on a job to make lace-trimmed collars and cuffs, and handkerchiefs for a dressmaker who catered to the wives of the chiefs of several factories that moved to our village from Kharkov and Leningrad. Soviet society always had class divisions, no matter what communism preached.

"As I was returning from this dressmaker's cottage to the other side of Rubtsovsk where we lived, a *buran*, a terrible storm, rose from the steppe. Snow was swirling up from the ground, down from the sky, blinding me and pushing me in every direction. I was exhausted from the long walk to the dressmaker's house, and furious because she hadn't paid me for my work. If I panicked, or sat down to rest, I'd be lost in the white maze and found—dead—days, weeks or months later. I mouthed silent prayers to God and pushed ahead in what I thought was the right direction. In a *buran* on the steppe, however, roads disappeared under huge drifts of snow.

"Suddenly the wind brought the sounds of a voice. At first I heard my name, then something else. I thought I was becoming delirious, but the voice and the words did not disappear. At last I heard 'Essinka, Essinka'—my nickname when I was little—followed by 'Sh'ma Israel!' As I came close I realized that Mama was standing in the middle of the road, homing me to safety with the words of our prayer, 'Hear, O Israel, the Lord Our God, the Lord is One.' "

After a short silence, Yakov turned to his students around the table. "We were never lost in a storm. No one has ever homed us with the Sh'ma . . . "

"Why then," I immediately asked, "are you all here in Jerusalem, at this table, studying Torah?"

The Ostrovs

One Sunday, some nine years ago, my phone rang early in the morning. An unusual time to receive a call in our house, except in case of emergency. I was very tense as I picked up the receiver. "Essinka, Essinka, is it you?" a nearly hysterical voice kept asking. In Russian, not English. "Who is it, who is it?" I responded in Polish. Language shock had set in. "This is Yulia Ostrov, daughter of Rebecca Abramovna Ostrov."

"Who is Rebecca Abramovna? I only know Aunt Zaya Ostrov, from Siberia!"

I changed from Polish to Russian, with English and Yiddish words thrown in. "Where are you?" I almost shouted, perhaps thinking the call came from Siberia. Or that it was part of the previous's night's dream.

"We're in Crown Heights, here in Brooklyn, with the

145

family of a distant cousin from Russia. Rebecca Abramovna *is* Aunt Zaya. That was her nickname when you knew her in Russia. I'm her daughter, and I have a daughter, too. Her name is Marina."

My head was swimming. "Where is Uncle Yozia?"

Yozia was Aunt Zaya's husband, neither of them related to us, but our guardian angels when we lived as deportees in Siberia. Uncle Yozia and Aunt Zaya were evacuated, not deported, to Rubtsovsk when the German army advanced on the Soviet Union. He had had a good position with a large industrial plant in Kharkov, which was transplanted in its entirety to the barren steppe of Siberia. He was a Soviet citizen of privilege, yet a conscientious Jew. They sustained us with their charm, their kindness, and in practical ways, too. When they got soap, they shared it with us several times. If their higher station in life, in the so-called classless society in the Soviet Union, entitled them to better food rations than my family got as capitalist deportees from Eastern Europe, they gave some to us.

Most of all, we loved them and they loved us.

When the war ended in 1945, Aunt Zaya and Uncle Yozia returned to central Russia and settled in Leningrad. That very same year they had a baby girl they named Yulia. We returned to Poland in 1946 as well and were reunited with Papa in Lodz upon his release from the army.

Before Yozia and Zaya left, they made up a code with Mama. If we ever left Poland for the United States, where Mama's brother lived, we'd write them that we went on a long visit to Benjamin. And we did go to America, and my mother wrote about our move in this oblique way. It was dangerous to receive mail from capitalist countries under Stalin's regime, especially for Jews; Jews were murdered by his henchmen for lesser offenses. Yozia would be in grave peril if we'd written from the United States.

"Why didn't you write to me? Didn't you ever get any of *my* letters?" My parents did not write, as Mama promised they wouldn't from America, but I did after I got married. Walter traveled widely as a concert pianist, and he mailed letters for me to Aunt Zaya and Uncle Yozia from "safe" countries: Switzerland, Norway, Sweden and Iceland. A return address, in care of his managers, was always included in my letters. No answers came. We lost contact with our beloved guardian angels.

But I did find a brother of Uncle Yozia's in Paris. He had defected from Russia sometime in the nineteen-thirties, while on a business mission to South America. Uncle Yozia had told Mama in Siberia that rumors and gossip, the only way one could get such news under Stalin, placed his brother somewhere in France.

As soon as I arrived in America, I looked in the New York telephone book and found the French consulate's address and number. Though I barely knew English or French, I called to ask whether I could come in and look through the Paris telephone directory. My sixth sense told me that Yozia's brother was living in Paris, and indeed there was an A. Ostrov in the book. I immediately wrote a long letter in Russian and asked whether he had a brother named Yozia, and what his parents' names were and other details.

I also told him that I had photographs that might be of his family, and if it was so, he should write to me forthwith.

A response quickly came; I sent the pictures and continued to write occasional notes. Sometimes they prompted an answer, sometimes they were ignored. After Walter and I were married we went on a trip to Europe, during which he played many concerts. In Paris, however, we were on vacation. I wanted to spend time with my beloved Uncle Yozia's brother.

After one meeting I realized that men can be brothers and not resemble each other in spirit. Perhaps one should not expect too much in such cases; no person can replace another exactly. My disappointment that there wasn't a replica of Uncle Yozia in Paris gnawed at me for a long time.

"Why didn't you answer my letters?" I repeated, thinking Yulia was still on the other end of the line. Aunt Zaya, whose voice is delicate, and has always been whispery, had taken the receiver. "Essinka, darling"—my name's Russian form of endearment—she kept saying, "Come, come to Brooklyn and we'll tell you everything." I could hardly believe this conversation was taking place on a normal December morning in New York.

Zaya put down the receiver, and someone who spoke excellent but heavily accented English gave me directions on how to reach the Ostrovs, who were the guests of a huge and incredibly generous Hassidic family on Empire Boulevard. When I hung up I was drenched in sweat and barely able to repeat the story to Walter, who stayed close to me throughout the conversation. He understood the outline of what was happening, having learned to translate languages he did not know from words culled here and there and my facial expressions.

I dressed quickly in warm slacks and a heavy sweater, clothes I normally don't wear when I go visiting, but it was cold and the subway trip from my apartment on the Upper West Side to Crown Heights in Brooklyn long. I ran to the train, not stopping to buy any gifts. I was afraid of bringing unsuitable presents of candy or cookies that were not sufficiently kosher, and the flower shops were still closed. I'd pick up something on Kingston Avenue in Brooklyn, right in the heart of the kosher bakeries and delicacy shops serving Crown Heights.

When I came out of the subway in front of the main Lubavitch synagogue on Eastern Parkway, I realized with horror that slacks were not acceptable attire for women in the Hassidic community. I considered going into a clothing store and buying a skirt, but I longed to get to Aunt Zaya, Yulia and Marina more than I wanted to adhere to the ultra-Orthodox dress code for women.

By the time I arrived at the address on Empire Boulevard given to me by the Ostrovs' hosts, every muscle in my body seemed in spasm. I wasn't sure just whom I'd find there: my dear, cozy Aunt Zaya, or a starchy, regal Rebecca Abramovna. Would Yulia be like her gentle, wonderful father? Was Marina a happy child? Would we get along after a nearly forty-year separation?

When I walked into the house of the Hassidic family, Aunt Zaya was standing close to the entrance. She looked like herself, but her hair was snow-white and her delicate face drawn and tired. Her green eyes were the same shade, but the light in them was extinguished. She still remembers that my first words to her that Sunday in Brooklyn were

"It *is* you!" as if I expected an imposter and did not believe she was real until we touched and hugged and cried together.

Yulia pressed me to her, then held me back at arm's length, looking at me as if I were a museum exhibit. "You know, Essinka, you were the heroine of my childhood." It was, almost, the most astonishing thing I'd heard that morning. Her parents were the heroes of my growing-up years in Siberia! How could I be hers?

Yulia told me that her father said I was the spunkiest, most fearless child he'd ever met. I, who was afraid of so much now, in middle age, was apparently not scared of anything in Siberia. Or so it seemed to Uncle Yozia.

Torrents of words from all three of us kept cascading while I was still in my coat. No one winced at my slacks when I took it off, though Yulia later said that they noticed. Marina skipped and danced and performed a Russian song, and the Lubavitch clan pressed food and drink on me from all sides. It was the happiest chaos I'd ever experienced.

When we sat down to talk in quiet, Yulia and Zaya told me that Uncle Yozia died in 1972, two years after my mother. "He always said that your mama was not only the smartest but the wisest person he'd ever met." Zaya nodded. "You know, Essinka, there's a difference between smartest and wisest!" Others had also said it of Mama.

Mama would have adored Yulia, a gentle, prematurely gray woman, with wise eyes herself, and her father's sweet nature. She and Aunt Zaya told me, sometimes in unison, sometimes in alternate sentences, why they did not write.

Uncle Yozia, Zaya and Yulia lived with a cousin of his after the war, cramped into small, cheerless rooms in Leningrad. The families had a disagreement. The Ostrovs moved, and the cousin remained angry. When letters came for them to the cousin's house, she destroyed them without telling anyone that mail arrived. Many years later, when she was ill, she confessed that some came from abroad, including many from Paris, which she suspected were from Uncle Yozia's brother. His name was not on the envelopes, but the handwriting seemed familiar.

Uncle Yozia was able to make contact with his brother before he died in 1972. And Yulia met her uncle after her father passed away. As a pediatrician, she was granted permission to visit France for a conference, and once there she saw him and his family. In 1970, Yozia, Zaya and Yulia vacationed in Vilna, the city where I was born, and they tried to find out if anyone there in the Jewish community knew of our whereabouts. It seems that after the war no one in Vilna even knew our name, though my family had lived there for many generations. The Ostrovs gave up looking for us, but only in Vilna.

After much agonizing, Yulia and Zaya decided to seek permission to emigrate to the West. But who would help them, send them affidavits? A distant cousin of Yulia's, an energetic, clever woman named Paulina, was part of a huge family, all of them members of the Lubavitch community in Brooklyn. Arrangements were made for them to claim Yulia, Marina and Zaya as their relatives also; visas were awaited interminably. Aunt Zaya got seriously ill. Yulia's husband did not even seek permission to emigrate. It would never have been granted. His work was too valuable to the Soviet government. He was a space program pilot and a translator of scientific papers from French, English and German on aerospace matters. (He was dismissed from his position and became a night guard in a small factory.) Time passed, tense and fraught with many dangers. But the Lubavitch family sent all the papers and guarantees and money for their tickets—how and through whom I still don't know—and the little trio of women, aged three to seventy, arrived in Brooklyn.

Yulia and Aunt Zaya immediately set about to look for us. Zaya vaguely, but correctly, remembered that my mother's brother lived in Brooklyn, but she did not remember Uncle Benjamin's name. What's more, even if she had, she would not have found him, for his death preceded their arrival by at least a decade. They checked my father's name in all the telephone directories: Brooklyn, Bronx, Queens, Staten Island. They called all the people who had names like my father's. None was right.

On Sunday when her call woke me, Yulia had the inspiration to try the Manhattan telephone directory. At first she and her hosts had little hope of finding us in Manhattan. They knew not a single soul who lived there. Manhattan was for business, for museums, theaters. Not a place where people like my family, Jewish people lived. Their idea, to me, seemed incongruous.

The first Rudomin Yulia called had a temporarily disconnected number. An automated operator answered and gave a number in Miami Beach, Florida. They called Florida that Sunday morning, even before they attempted other Rudomins in Manhattan. The number was my father's! He was not at all surprised. He said that he had always expected that the Ostrovs would get out of Russia, though he never mentioned this to me. Papa welcomed them to America, gave them my married name and telephone number. He was eighty-three years old when all of this transpired one wintry Sunday morning in New York. The good Lord gave him long years for many purposes. One of them surely was to connect us with the Ostrovs, forty years after we had all left Siberia. Had he, God forbid, not lived to an old, old age, we might never have seen each other again. The Ostrovs had no way of knowing my married name, thanks to the cousin who threw out my letters.

I wanted to ask, but couldn't bring myself to cast aspersions on Uncle Yozia's brother, why he did not tell them of my existence? Perhaps he forgot my letters and visit, but surely he saved his brother's and mother's pictures that I'd sent. Life isn't perfect. "Pinch your cheeks, my child, and get on with it"—my mother's apt words often ring in my ears.

At the Lubavitch family's table in Crown Heights everyone was quiet, listening to our stories and what providence has granted us. Had it not been for them, that wonderfully generous, close-knit family, and the whole Lubavitch community, Aunt Zaya, who was so good to me in Siberia, her daughter and granddaughter would still be in the Soviet Union.

After many years of great difficulty in renewing her medical license, Yulia is at last a practicing doctor in the Boston area. Marina is as American as any Yankee could be. Probably more so—she works at it. Aunt Zaya, who still doesn't speak much English, thinks America is the greatest land in the world. She can say anything, do anything, has her own kitchen—not one she has to share with other families as she had to in Leningrad—and the supermarket shelves have endless variety. For people who've stood in long lines for everything, from a loaf of bread and a small bag of sugar to a bar of soap and bathroom paper, being able to buy all this, and much more, by just walking into a store is equal to paradise.

Heaven comes in various guises.

Nahum

Nahum saved my life. Not figuratively speaking, but quite literally.

He and his father, Avrom, were together with us in Siberia during the war. His mother was visiting Palestine at the time of our arrests and deportations. I knew a number of people from Vilna, including my uncle Sioma, who went there as tourists in the late 1930s. While we froze on the endless steppe, she broiled under the merciless sun of the Middle East. Neither was conducive to good health and peace of mind during World War II. Each worried for the other.

Nahum was a boy of fifteen or sixteen when we arrived in Siberia. He was neither tall nor short, neither handsome nor homely. His skin was pockmarked, or perhaps scarred by acne, a disorder I'd only learn about years later in America. His dark, straight hair was nearly always disheveled, as if a strong Siberian wind blew right through it and Nahum did not trouble to comb it after the storm. His eyes, however, were always focused on the person with whom he was speaking; they were thoughtful, kind, dark eyes. He seemed at all times calm, serene, trusting.

It was not possible for him and me, at eleven a mere child in his eyes, to have anything in common. His father, Avrom, and I had much more to talk about—and did.

Avrom, Abraham in English, was an educator and journalist in Vilna, with a fine reputation in Jewish cultural circles, a reputation that continued to grow after the war ended and he began to write once more. How and why he and his son were deported with capitalists and enemies of the people seemed an aberration, for his means were average and his political leanings, I should guess, to the left of center. This aberration, however, saved their lives.

They came to Siberia in sorrier shape than all the rest of us did. They didn't possess an extra pair of shoes, slacks or even a shirt. What's more, the two men were entirely unable to look after their needs. Neither Nahum nor Avrom had any idea of how to plant a garden, make a fire, cook a meal, sew on a button, darn a hole. Both looked in perpetual need of someone's caring hand and a "home-cooked" meal, even if that meal merely consisted of inventively prepared potatoes.

My mother's specialty in Siberia, and even afterward when we could cook anything we liked, was called *tekla*. Why it had this name is buried in ancient family folklore, but I believe it came from a family servant who prepared it and whose name had become synonymous with this dish.

When we had potatoes, onions and a bit of oil or other fat all at the same time, Mama cooked *tekla*. The onions were fried to an almost burnt crispness, the potatoes were boiled in their skins, peeled, cut into cubes and added to the onions in the pan. All was mixed and fried some more, until it smelled almost as good as *cholent*, the traditional Sabbath dish. Especially to those with empty stomachs. Mama tried to cook *tekla* each time Nahum and Avrom came to visit. But no matter what was in our pot, there was always enough to share with these good men.

After our meals together, Mama would ask indirectly about Avrom's supply of onions and potatoes. Wasn't it a terrible winter? Everyone's vegetables froze in their dug-out cellars. How were theirs? Were they fortunate, as we were, to get their oil rations? They must take a little; we have enough for now. Surely a new supply will soon arrive from Tashkent or Samarkand—or the moon, I'd mutter silently, and feel instantly ashamed.

Avrom argued that they had all they needed, Nahum sat silently at the table, I scraped off and ate the leftover onions and potatoes from the bowl, and Mama quietly went about gathering a little parcel of meager provisions.

Sometimes Mama lightly suggested that Avrom bring over clothing that needed patching and mending. Both she and I were skilled in turning collars, darning holes, fixing hems. She tried, delicately, to help them preserve whatever was still wearable. Strangely enough, I really enjoyed this work. I still would, but darned socks are not "in" at the moment, and cuffs on today's shirts cannot be turned.

To assure their self-respect and honor, and to help my grades in school, Mama asked Nahum and Avrom to help me with algebra, geometry and science homework. I was hopeless in all three, and was always either failing or on the verge of failing.

Even in our small Siberian village schooling was rigorous, teachers demanding, curriculum on a high level. Certainly too high for the imbecile in math and science that I was, and have remained for the rest of my life. Those of us who lived in Siberia were the only ones not shocked when *Sputnik* took off. Soviet schools educated their young well, even in Siberia, even during the war—in a way, possibly *because* of the war, when many experienced teachers from universities in Leningrad, Moscow, Kiev and other large European cities were evacuated to distant parts of the Soviet Union, including little outposts on the steppe.

Nahum's and Avrom's ministrations to waken the brain cells in my head that Mama thought were dormant, and I knew were dead, were entirely unsuccessful. Throughout my later schooling in Poland and in New York, I have had to face the same problem. My parents thought language changes were at fault. I knew better—and so did my well-meaning but thwarted teachers.

In the Brooklyn high school that I'd attended for one year after arriving from Europe I had a wonderful chemistry teacher. I did not understand one word he said, but I diligently prepared my assignments, attended class, was scrupulously attentive, though mystified at the goings-on in the laboratory and the discussions held by his students. Bernard Jaffe passed me with the lowest mark, but he passed me.

Years later, that same wonderful teacher wrote a book called *Chemistry Creates a New World*, which was published by the company for which I worked. In the late 1950s I took him to lunch—he was the first man whose lunch I had paid for in New York, and he was as miserable about it as I was in his class. I asked whether he remembered me, and told him my maiden name. "Of course I remember you. You were the worst student I ever had." We got along splendidly nevertheless.

After a certain point, in Siberia, I had to accept the fact that Nahum had simply given up on me. His "tutorials" ceased. Avrom and I, however, forged a bond on a different subject: writing.

He told me stories from Yiddish literature that I could not get in Siberia. The library in our tiny village had a remarkable collection—translations of Shakespeare by Boris Pasternak, of novels by Alexandre Dumas, Charles Dickens's *Little Dorrit, Oliver Twist, Dombey and Son*, not to mention Pushkin, Dostoyevsky, Tolstoy, Turgenev, Gorky. But there were no stories by Sholem Aleichem, Mendele Moicher Sforim, I. L. Peretz, nor works by any of the poets who were writing in Vilna in the 1920s and 1930s. Avrom knew them by heart and would recite some for my pleasure and education in Yiddish literature.

I would show him essays I wrote for the school "paper." This was, in fact, merely a large board in school on which reporters, such as I, would nail down contributions. Avrom liked them. Since he was an educator in Vilna, his opinion mattered enormously to me. I also showed him poems and stories I wrote whenever I had had a clean piece of paper on which to copy my work. Most of the time we had to write homework assignments over old newspapers or other "recycled" paper. Writing final drafts of poetry and stories on such paper made me miserable. A blank white page is what I craved. I still do, but I am still very, very careful about wasting paper whenever I write.

Late one afternoon, after Papa had been in the army for over a year, Avrom and I were alone, waiting for Mama to return from her factory job in Rubtsovsk. I think Avrom worked the night shift at that time. We sat by a little table near the window in the last of our Siberian huts. The day before, I'd written a long narrative poem and copied it out, with a feeling of luxury, onto a sleek piece of lined paper. I was too nervous about his opinion to leave him alone, and even more nervous about being present when he read it. I paced the little room, not daring to look directly at his face, yet stealing glances to see his expression. Finally I sat down across from him at the table, my head in my hands.

He came over to me and, standing sideways, put his hand on my shoulder. "Some day," he said, "you'll be a writer." Not, you may be a writer—you *will* be a writer is what he said. I looked at his hand on my shoulder, then I looked up at his face. I remember the serious look in his eyes; I also recall that his shirt cuff was in shreds and would need mending again.

I often think of Avrom, even when I write how-to books, with hemming, sewing and other mundane instructions. I remembered him when I translated I. L. Peretz stories from Yiddish into English, and when they were published in America, a long way from Siberia.

Avrom lived long enough to know that his prediction proved right. I only wonder if he'd remembered it as well as I do, or even remembered it at all. In a way, not only Nahum, but his father saved my life. His faith gave me hope.

When the war was over and our exile in Siberia was finally ending, we got permission to return to Poland. Mama, Grandmother and I were to join Papa in Lodz. Avrom and Nahum planned to go to Lodz, too, and eventually be reunited with their wife and mother. Her letters occasionally reached them in Siberia, all the way from Palestine. Actually, the distance was not as insurmountable as it may seem on paper. One could get to Palestine from our tiny village in Siberia through Soviet Asia: Alma Ata, Tashkent, Samarkand, then via Iran and Egypt, all the way to Tel Aviv, Haifa or Jerusalem, not by air but by land and sea. Perhaps Avrom and Nahum might have gotten permission to go to Palestine instead of Lodz, but fortunately for me they were on the train which took us to Poland, even in the same car to which we were assigned.

The train was composed of many cars usually assigned for shipping cattle. The Soviets called it an "echelon"; they used it not only to transport people like us but soldiers who went to the front, and those fortunate enough to return home at the end of the war.

The mood on our train was at times exuberant with relief that the war was over, that we were on the way to a "normal" life, but it was also a period of great anxiety. We'd heard reports of the Nazi slaughter in Europe, but in my heart I'd hoped against hope that it was not really all true, that it was a nightmare from which I'd wake up once we came to Poland.

Margola, Liusik, Grandmother; Mussik, Sanna, their mother; Reisunia and Salik, their parents; Aunt Sonitchka, her baby and husband; Uncle Sioma, his wife and baby girl; Uncle Dodzia, his wife and son; my Bobbe Reise and her daughters Rivkah, Leah, Yocha, her son Yankl, their husbands, wives, children, their children's children, who were not only my cousins but beloved friends; my mother's aunts Nadia, Fania, Lisa, Uncle Reuven, their husbands, wife, their children and their children's children, they could not *all* be dead. It seemed too monstrous to be true. I sent out beseeching thoughts to Heaven as the train was moving toward Poland. Heaven listened, but not to the pleas I sent its way. It acted in its own mysterious manner.

The train on which we traveled made stops at stations where women carrying baskets sold sheep's milk cheese and black bread and other simple provisions. We also stopped for hours on sidings, in the midst of nowhere, along open fields and dense forests. After other, more important transports passed us, we would chug on. One day the train stopped on a completely isolated stretch along the beautiful, rough-edged Ural Mountains. Snow covered the ground, but the flat, treeless steppe was far behind us. Before me were evergreens covering breathtaking vistas. Crystals sparkled in sunlight like in a Russian fairy tale illustrated by Afanasiev, not in a book, but in real life, in front of my eyes.

I had to get out of the stale, dark cattle car, to breathe fresh air and be in sunlight. The sliding door was slightly ajar and the ladder, on which we climbed up and down to the ground, was in place. Mama was asleep; she was making up for endless sleepless nights during our exile. I asked Grandmother's permission to leave the train. She, ever ready for adventure, saw no reason to forbid me the pleasure.

I put on my new jacket and boots and went down to the embankment. No house, no sign of smoke from a chimney, no animal tracks in the snow were visible from any direction. I shouted hello to people who stood in the doors of other cars in the train. Then I trudged toward the front because I knew someone who traveled in a car close to the locomotive.

Suddenly the train whistle blew several times, which meant that we would move on within a few seconds. Fear paralyzed me. Someone yelled that I should climb into their car, but I was afraid that Grandmother and Mama would be hysterical if I was not back when the train left the siding. As I ran like a jackrabbit toward our car, the train began to move and to pick up speed. I saw myself left on the siding, alone, deserted, in the middle of the Urals, eaten by wolves or frozen to death, my skeleton discovered decades later.

In the midst of this slow-motion, phantasmagoric dream, I suddenly saw a familiar figure running toward me. I felt myself being lifted around my knees and thrown head first into our railroad car. When I got up, dazed but nearly unbruised, I realized it was Nahum who'd saved my life. He had looked out of the open door, realized my predicament, jumped out and run toward me.

There was no time for Nahum to climb into our car after me. The train was moving faster and faster with every passing second. There were no alarm handles to pull, no conductors who could stop the train. A nightmare had come to life.

Mama, Grandmother, Avrom, all the passengers in our car were stunned. It had happened so quickly. No one spoke, shouted, blamed me, blamed each other. Like a frame of film frozen on the screen. Silent. Without background music.

After what seemed like hours, but probably was less than a minute, everyone talked. When the train made the next stop, someone would notify the engineer, the train would go back and look for Nahum. Surely we would find him. I must have looked so stricken that Avrom put his hand on my shoulder, just as he'd done when he read my poem.

No one thought to look through the still-open door when the train began to pick up speed and I was sprawled on the floor. If someone had done so before closing the door, we'd have seen Nahum hanging on for dear life at the end of the train, on a cabooselike car with a tall and sturdy ladder.

Luckily the train stopped again after only a few hours. By the time someone opened our door, Nahum was ready to climb in on the ladder. He was blue from exposure, his hands hardly moved, his teeth clattered like the wheels of the train. But he was alive and back in our car. I was so relieved I sobbed for hours. No word of reproof, of anger toward me, the cause of his misery, escaped Nahum's lips. He accepted Mama's and Grandmother's thanks, my blubbering gratitude, congratulations and slaps on the shoulder from others with calmness and equanimity, as was his nature.

Today he is still the calm, unpretentious, natural boy I knew in Siberia and saw later in Lodz. He's not a boy, of course, except to me. He lives in Toronto, with his Warsaw-born wife, Henia. They have two children—a son who is a physician and a daughter who has a Ph.D. in literature and teaches at a university not too far from Toronto. Nahum and Henia are grandparents; I have pictures of their grandchildren on my shelves.

Nahum is a typesetter for Jewish publications; Henia teaches in the I. L. Peretz School, where Yiddish is part of the curriculum and where half the school day's lessons are conducted in that rich language. Her Yiddish accent is unlike Nahum's and mine, but she's one of "ours" by now, a Vilna native by marriage if not by birth. Avrom and his wife, Nahum's mother, who returned from Palestine to join them in Europe, lived for many years near Nahum and his family. Avrom wrote articles and essays after the war; his wife was active in Yiddish cultural circles as well.

Since I'd written briefly of Nahum, in *The Endless Steppe*, I receive letters from readers asking what had become of my rescuer. Many ask whether I felt, and still feel, guilty about his nearly fatal deed of kindness. I write to tell them that I did and still do. I copy these letters and send them to Nahum. He seems to enjoy them; he responds with jests and genuine modesty. When we speak, he brushes away all references to his deed, as if it were just part of a day's work, something as simple and natural as setting a headline in twenty-four point type for his paper.

Occasionally he comes to New York. Occasionally I go to Toronto. I'd take the train more often, but travel does not come easily to me. He knows and understands the reasons better than anyone.

Miss Rachel

It was sunny the morning she came to our house. Sunshine and happiness, bright light and cool breezes. That's how I recall it.

I was in bed when the door opened and a young woman, with rosy cheeks like McIntosh apples, walked into my room. I looked up suspiciously from under my blanket. That is how the once young woman, now over fifty years older, remembers it also.

She introduced herself as Panna Rachela (Miss Rachel in Polish) and said she had come to be my teacher and friend. Not governess, which carried unwelcome authority, but someone to learn from, play with and love.

Miss Rachel wore a cheerful blouse, though I don't recall its color and pattern. She also wore a dark skirt, silk stockings and pretty shoes. Not the cotton hose and sensible oxfords that were worn by other governesses I knew.

Her hair was short and straight. There is little left of it as she's gotten older. She was not beautiful in a conventional sense, but she was beautiful to me when I first saw her, and she is beautiful now each time I'm with her in Israel.

Her deep brown eyes, behind round, steel-rimmed spectacles, sparkled as she came closer and sat on the edge of my bed. She rolled down the blanket from under my chin and smoothed my tangled hair and worried forehead. Her hand was cool and calming. Mama had the perspicacity to let the two of us meet without her introduction or presence, a gesture as wise as it was considerate.

The previous governess I'd had was named Miss Dora. I disliked her dour face and sour expression, her long, wrinkled neck and piercing voice. She acted like a drill sergeant, commandeering not only me, but some of my cousins. Every hour of each day was scheduled: meals, lessons, play, walks, rest periods. Punctuality and neatness were essential. Though I was only five, I remember it well.

One day after my midmorning meal, I ran off to find Mama. Miss Dora remained at the small table in my room. She was especially dictatorial that morning, making me finish the last bit of food on my plate and insisting that I complete a project we started that morning before I could play with my cousin Mussik.

Mama was getting ready for one of her classes or charity tasks and was braiding her long hair in front of the mirror. I said that she could punish me as much as she liked, but I would never again obey Miss Dora. I would not draw pictures, nor go for walks, nor do gymnastics under her direction.

Mama knew when she'd lost a battle even before it had

really begun. From earliest childhood I'd had a streak of stubbornness no one could break, though many had tried. She, in her wisdom, let me win sometimes if it mattered to me and caused me no harm. Instead of arguing, Mama recited a witty ditty in Polish about a girl named Zosia Samosia, who knew what was best, and who would and could do everything for herself, by herself, on her own, entirely alone. Like a big lady. That ditty, which I can still recite but don't, broke the tension. I'd win my case, but not in a spirit of battle.

Miss Dora soon disappeared from our house, and Miss Rachel came to spend each weekday from breakfast through supper with me. She was my teacher, companion, friend and protector. She was not Mama's replacement, she was her extension.

Miss Rachel praised me if I deserved it. Mama was far more stingy with compliments. Miss Rachel and I made a chart on which we pasted stars for every day of the week. Gold stars were for A + days, silver stars were for A days, red, blue and green stars rated the rest of my behavior and accomplishments. Perhaps such a chart would not meet child-rearing standards now, but I loved the weeks that had more gold stars than others, and I tried hard to deserve them.

Miss Rachel's own life had not been easy. While with us she fell in love with the son of a prosperous electric-company owner from a neighboring town, one of my father's best clients. Miss Rachel's position in the social strata was considered far below that of the man she loved, though she had received her diploma from the best Polish gymnasium in Vilna, where she was a brilliant student and the only Jew in her class. She came from a family with limited means, and to make things even more difficult, two of her brothers dabbled in communism and one was jailed for his antigovernment activities. For her to marry the son of a prominent Jewish businessman could cause harm. Class distinctions, alas, were not restricted to royalty. When Mama and I talked of it years later, she'd get as angry as I'd ever seen her.

Rachel did marry the man she loved, in secret, and she continued to teach and take care of me and to live in her own mother's house. I knew none of that, of course, in the beginning. Some years later, when Rachel got pregnant, her father-in-law invited her to join the family enclave in their town near Vilna. She returned to our house before the birth of her baby. Mama looked after Rachel, prepared her favorite foods and bought her delicacies—as if she were a beloved sister.

Miss Rachel named her firstborn Esther, and oddly enough her husband's name was Samuel, like my father's. For fifty years I had thought, and said, that Miss Rachel told everyone that when she married, her husband's name would be Samuel, and that her first baby would be a girl and that she would name her Esther. In Israel, in 1988, I learned from her that it was I who'd said it ever since I was five.

The war broke out soon after Rachel's baby was born and she returned with her to her husband's family. The Germans were approaching from the west, the Soviets from the east. The Russian army occupied the small town where Rachel lived before the Germans could reach it.

Before the relative hiatus of peace was over, during the days of the pact between Hitler and Stalin, Rachel and her family were deported to Siberia. A year or so later, the same fate befell us. It saved all of us, of course, but at the time neither Rachel and her family, nor we, considered it a favor from Above.

Rachel told me in 1988, in Jerusalem, that she wrote to Mama from Siberia to Vilna and received a reply just before we, too, were deported. Mama must have remembered Rachel's address and sent a letter to her from Rubtsovsk, though I have no recollection of this correspondence.

And so, as a consequence, a surreal, dreamlike event took place one summer day in the mid-1940s while we were in one small outpost and Rachel in another part of the vast steppe of Russia. Her father-in-law, who also knew of our whereabouts, had heard that a truck driver from their village was heading for ours to deliver a shipment of goods, the nature of which she has by now forgotten. He told Rachel, and she, on sudden impulse, went straight to the truck driver and asked him to take her along.

She got no police authorization for travel—an absolute necessity in those days—she did not know how long the trip would take, and she did not know the driver. All immense obstacles, ignored at great risk. Nevertheless, the truck driver took a fancy to her crazy mission, her spunk, and said he'd take her along. They rode for many hours, in an old truck, on bumpy roads, toward an endless horizon.

Like a mirage, Miss Rachel appeared in our hut in Siberia. I could hardly believe it then; I can hardly believe it now. She brought me several skeins of Mouline embroidery yarn—pink, blue and eggshell—which I kept in my sewing box for years; proof that her visit took place. Then I hid it for ever greater safety. That place is so safe, even I can no longer find it, though I've looked diligently through dozens of boxes.

I included this Bergman-movie-like sequence in *The Endless Steppe*, my story of our years in Siberia, but my editor suggested that I remove it. It seemed to her so amazing that she doubted readers would believe me. The omission hurt Miss Rachel deeply, and she was not reticent about expressing her disappointment.

After the war we met, by chance, in Lodz. That city seemed to draw many Jews returning from exile in Siberia. By then Rachel and her husband had two little boys, as well as Esther who was seven.

Rachel's Esther and I are good friends now. She is the producer of one of the most widely heard radio programs on Kol Israel, and the winner of many broadcasting awards in her country. During one of her visits to New York, Eti (as she is now called by friends and family) said she was prepared to hate me from childhood on. Somehow it did not work out that way, though her reasons for wanting to hate me were fully understandable. No matter what she did as a child, I had done better—according to her mother. I was a serene, if stubborn, child; she was stormy. She was messy; I was neat. I spoke quietly; she was loud. Or so Eti quotes her mother.

When speaking to me of her children, Rachel has always seemed incredibly proud of all three, but most particularly of her daughter. Eti says that Miss Rachel was never lavish with praise nor with any overt sign that she'd felt *naches*, a sense of pride, at all Eti had accomplished. I've told Eti on more than one occasion that each of us could have fared worse.

Since our meeting in Lodz in 1946, Miss Rachel and I saw each other a few times when Walter and I were in Israel in 1950. She scrutinized my brand-new husband over the top of her ubiquitous steel-rimmed spectacles and only half-jokingly ordered him to be good to me. "She's mine, too, you know." I saw Rachel again in 1968 when I took my daughter to meet her, and Grandmother Anna, who lived near Tel Aviv. When we came in 1978 to celebrate our son's bar mitzvah, Miss Rachel and her whole family were part of our celebration. Though personal visits have been far too rare, our bond and devotion have never slackened.

I saw Miss Rachel last in 1988, when Walter and I spent many weeks in Jerusalem. Rachel's husband had by then died, her two sons were in opposite political camps, and she seemed tense. Her younger boy is a settler on the West Bank; the older son lives in Jerusalem. Both have children; the older son's daughter had just completed military duty. Two boys, still in high school, were facing four years in the army.

The younger son is a member of the Likud party, a hard-liner though not a fanatic. He won't let Rachel visit for fear she'll be hurt, but he has no intention of moving and giving up his home and land. He can no longer communicate with some members of his family. They disagree on political issues, and issues of this kind are not taken lightly even at a family dinner table.

Eti has the opposite view. She has written and broadcast a series of seminal, award-winning programs, understanding of Arabs and their relations with Jews. She wants peace, she tries to understand and present both points of view. She loves both her brothers, one a hard-liner, the other somewhere between her point of view and his, but their political differences are basic and visceral. Miss Rachel is caught in the verbal crossfire among her children. One day she agrees with Eti, the next time her West Bank son's point of view prevails.

Rachel and I did not talk only about politics during our visits. That isn't what brought us together. Her youth and my childhood in Vilna are our main topics when we are alone. She has said several times that being with me makes her feel young, as if she were nineteen again. I wish I'd feel as if I were five.

On a day-long visit in October of 1988, we were totally undisturbed in her snug and color-filled rooms in a remote Jerusalem suburb. Handmade pillows, needlepoint pictures, books and more books covered nearly every surface in Rachel's apartment. She served a spare lunch, did not put too much on the table, nor did she urge me to finish what I put on my plate. A point of pride with her, it seemed, was the fact that she never made me eat more than I wanted—and, she said triumphantly, I was a "lazy eater." Her voice and her manner implied, perhaps inadvertently, a disagreement with my family's usual exhortations: EAT! She did not follow their example in Vilna, nor years later in Jerusalem.

As if she'd heard my mental detection, Rachel said quickly, "Your mother never criticized me. We discussed matters as equals. Only once we had a 'to-do' that still makes me blush." Rachel told me the story.

Our maid had taken the afternoon off, and my parents were expected somewhere for supper. Mama asked Rachel whether she'd agree to prepare my evening meal. Rachel would not; it was not her duty to cook, she told Mama. She was expected to teach me, keep me company, she'd stay until the housekeeper returned, but she would not cook. " 'Very well,' your Mama said and telephoned the office to tell your Papa that she'd be late. She put one of her wonderful aprons over her elegant dress and went to the kitchen without further ado. She prepared omelets for you and for me and served them to us at the dining-room table. As she was leaving, she turned to me with her wonderful smile and remarked, 'When you get married, I'll have to tell your husband that you don't even know how to make scrambled eggs.' "

Rachel hit her forehead with the palm of her hand, fifty-three years later in the suburbs of Jerusalem, while we ate hard-boiled eggs at her kitchen table. "Tell me more, Rokh-elle," which is my favorite nickname for her. "I want to know everything that you can remember." Though I did not feel like a small child, I sounded like one as I begged for just "one more story."

She told me about her beloved sister Betya who was ill with TB while Miss Rachel was part of our family. When she returned from a sanatorium in western Poland, near Zakopane, which is famous for its wonderful climate, Mama insisted that Betya spend the summer with us. " 'There will be enough room,' your Mama told us, 'and lots of rich food.

It'll be good for you and for Betya.' " Betya completed her
recuperation with us; several years later, she was killed by
the Nazis.

Miss Rachel considered my mother's invitation an act of
bravery, not to mention great kindness. She took in Betya
on faith; how could she have been sure that Betya was well
enough to join a family with children? All of us, Mussik,
Sanna, other cousins, were with us that summer in Volo-
kumpia, where we ran in the woods and played by the river.
"She followed in the footsteps of her own mother," Rachel
said in a low voice. She adored my grandmother when we
were young and revered her memory as if she was part of
her own family. "I'll tell you a story about your mama's
mother. I don't think you know it." I didn't and will be
forever grateful that Rokhelle did.

"Your grandmother came from a small town named Ivia;
she moved to Vilna when she married your grandfather. A
young Jewish girl in that small town fell in love with a
dashing Polish officer, left her family, married him and
converted to Catholicism. Her family sat *shivah*, in mourning, as if she had died, and no one in or from Ivia would
speak to her or acknowledge her existence.

"Except your grandmother!" Rachel held up her right
index finger and pointed it in my face, as if otherwise I
would not comprehend the importance of her story. "Your
grandmother received her in her home whenever this young
woman came to visit Vilna. She made her welcome. She
never abandoned her."

Rachel always knew, she said, when the young woman's
husband also came to Vilna, on army duty or for pleasure,

as the couple did not live in our city even after they moved away from Ivia. "A large basket of elaborately wrapped delicacies would appear on your grandmother's sideboard, with the officer's calling card tucked in the front."

Rachel sighed. It got chilly in the room, but I'm not sure whether it was because the sun had set, or because of what she had told me. Did it really matter? Grandmother was dead, Margola went to her death with her, Liusik was dead, so many for whom she set such an excellent example were gone. But the story lives on.

It was getting very dark and Miss Rachel began fussing that I ought to call a taxi to take me back to the center of Jerusalem where we stayed. I refused; the bus seemed the right way to travel, as if I truly belonged to the people of the city I love. And I was not yet ready to leave.

"Show me your *hand arbeit*," I asked Rachel. I wanted to see her handiwork projects, which is what those Yiddish words mean. Rachel opened cabinets stuffed to overflowing with leftover fabrics, shirts on which the collars were worn, but from which she still made pretty party napkins or guest towels. She made many for Eti's newly renovated apartment in Tel Aviv and for her sons' homes. Surely Rachel could have afforded a few lengths of new fabric. That, however, is not in her nature, nor is it in mine. Nothing's to be thrown out if it can be recycled. In Vilna she made dresses for my dolls using leftover materials from various projects. While we flipped through her remnants, she asked whether I recalled Heidi's bright red gabardine dress that had . . . I finished her sentence by describing my doll's dress in minutest detail: a yoke on top, with pleats down the back and the front, tiny round mother-of-pearl buttons and a tailored collar. Rachel nodded; we looked at each other in wonder at our total recall of a doll's dress so long, long ago.

She took out boxes of embroidery floss in a rainbow of colors. I searched for skeins made by Mouline in France such as those she'd given me in Siberia, but there were none. I asked if I could have one or two of her DMC brand embroidery floss skeins. "Take twenty," she said. "Take thirty, take all of them!" I took three of nearly the identical colors she brought me in Siberia. She also gave me a pair of crocheted blue baby booties for a new baby I might know. "I know one," I told Miss Rachel. "A little girl who lives in Rhode Island."

As Rachel hurried to get me on the bus back to the center of town, she asked whether I knew of a good way to decorate old tin boxes where she'd put cookies she planned to bake as Hanukkah gifts. At first I thought she was teasing. One of the first teachers to show me how to make something from nothing was asking me how to decorate tin boxes? On a dark street in Jerusalem? She was absolutely serious. No smile seemed to cross her face.

"You take dried beans and peas, and differently shaped noodles, and get good strong white glue," I said. "Then arrange all of these into a nice pattern and glue them to the top of the box, but not to the sides. They'll come unglued if you put them on the sides. Remember that." We were nearly by the bus stop. "Then," I said, "you'll have to get a good spray paint. Is it available in Jerusalem?"

Rachel seemed unsure. "Spray paint? What kind? The kind you use to paint a car?"

"No, Rokhelle, not a car. The kind that comes in small cans and bright colors. Silver, bronze, gold, red, blue. Children in America can no longer use them in school. The fumes are too strong." It sounded like instructions in one of the craft books I'd written.

My bus, number 18, *chai* for life, and my favorite number, the date on which I was born and my parents married, was approaching. It was almost at the stop and I was still describing to Rachel how to paint tin boxes that she'd fill with cookies for Hanukkah. I got on the bus, yelled through the window that I would write and send other ideas. "I'll come back! I will see you soon!" I shouted before the bus turned the corner.

Some higher forces must have planned such a parting. How else could I have said good-bye to my Rokhelle without coming unglued on all sides, in front of people on the number 18 bus in Jerusalem?

Bobbe Reise

Two events in my great-grandmother's long life are so powerful and miraculous that all else she'd lived through and accomplished pales beside them.

In the late 1920s she engaged a scribe to write a Torah in her house. It took many months or a year to complete writing the Five Books of Moses on parchment, using special quills and ink and following all necessary religious ritual to complete the holy task. A fire broke out in her home when the Torah was completed. She saved the Scriptures from flames and smoke while many of her other possessions were destroyed. Mama told me that she did this at the risk of her life.

In 1941, after the Nazis occupied Vilna, Great-grandmother decided to cheat them of the satisfaction of killing another Jew. She would not be led to death in Ponar, or be summarily shot on the street.

By sheer willpower and tenacity she chose the day of her death. She did not commit suicide, a grave sin for a Jew. She was observant as well as descended from a long line of rabbis. She was eighty-nine or ninety—no one knew the date or year she was born. But everyone who knew her in Vilna in 1941 remembers that this was the year Bobbe Reise died.

That day came soon after the Nazis began their systematic annihilation of Jews in the Jerusalem of Lithuania. The S.S. began daily roundups of people, shot them on the streets or in the headquarters of the Gestapo. Truckloads of people went to Ponar, others were killed in a random manner or shipped westward to camps in Poland and Germany, Latvia and Estonia.

Great-grandmother's oldest son, Yankl, and her brilliant grandson, Elik, were caught on the street and summarily shot. When she learned what happened to her son and her grandson, she saw what was to come for them all and she made her decision. My mother's cousin, the youngest daughter of Great-grandmother's youngest daughter, who survived the Holocaust, told me the story.

Several days after Yankl and Elik were killed, Great-grandmother announced to her family that she, too, was going to die. She decided that it would happen that very day, late in the evening. No one could dissuade her, she said, so they shouldn't try. She had made up her mind.

She laid out her *tachrichim*, the shroud in which she wished to be buried, prepared a large candle from some secret cache to put beside her body, and gave instructions for her burial. Everyone assumed she was so distraught that she did not know what she was saying. Suicide never entered anyone's thoughts. It would not permit her to be buried in consecrated ground, near her family, as she had decreed.

Yet, that very evening, after washing herself fastidiously in the cramped quarters the family occupied, she went early to bed—and died in her sleep. She did it with the same deliberation and dignity that she'd displayed in abundance during her life. She even received a decent burial. Astonishingly, the family was able to escort her body to a resting place, like that of her husband, whose death had preceded hers by more than sixty years. The Jewish population had not yet been herded into the ghetto and the cemetery near Vilna had not yet been destroyed.

My mother's cousin's face reflects disbelief, pride and respect when she speaks of this astonishing event, even half a century later. In death, as in life, Great-grandmother was awesome.

Bobbe means grandmother in Yiddish. In English Reise would be called Rose. Her name suited her; thorny as the stem of a rose, imposing as the flower when it reaches full bloom. She was called Bobbe Reise by her grandchildren and great-grandchildren and by relatives who were not linked to her by blood.

She did not resemble the typical *bobbe* of East European tradition. She wasn't a charming, plump little lady with round cheeks, white curls hidden beneath a babushka, jolly eyes and a chirpy voice urging everyone to eat. Her hair, even in her eighties, was only sprinkled with gray, her slightly wrinkled face did not indicate old age, but wisdom and authority.

Bobbe Reise was tall, lean, severe, elegantly dressed. Her clothes were impeccably cut, conservative and as appropriate for the 1990s as they were in the 1890s and in the 1930s when I knew her. Her flared skirts moved when she strode across a room, and I recall her blouses and dresses being creamy and soft when I brushed against them. Her business was textiles; she sold and used only the best.

Even her jewelry is memorable, not because it was large, but because she almost always wore the same little pins and earrings, her wedding ring and a watch, and not much else. She put on a long rope of real pearls for special events. Everything about Bobbe Reise was understated, save for her personality. Her voice was firm and sometimes dictatorial. She brooked no nonsense, even from those she loved best. Even now, at age ninety, my father refers to Bobbe Reise with affection and respect as a "difficult passenger," or "heavy luggage."

Family history has it that she was married between her thirteenth and fourteenth birthdays. That must have been around the year 1865. Her husband, Hillel Cunzer, was a very young widower with a small daughter. He was a successful merchant and came from a family that included Avrom Cunzer, the Learned Jew in the Court of the Czar, and the great Badchen, Eliakum Cunzer, who created and performed songs, ballads and epics at ceremonial occasions throughout Eastern Europe and later in America.

Teachers, rabbis, judges in Jewish courts of law, were all part of Great-grandfather's huge clan. Bobbe Reise never missed an opportunity to remind us of our *yiches*, our heritage, our ancestors, and our obligations to live up to their standards. When a distant relative or in-law did not behave according to her strict standards, her worst invective was: "Ha! This one is not *ours*!"

At a very young age, Bobbe Reise not only cared for the little girl her husband brought to the marriage but bore in quick succession three sons and three daughters of her own. Great-grandfather died of heart failure while still in his thirties, leaving his young wife with seven small children.

Bobbe Reise took over the family business after he died, and raised the children in Lubtch, a small town near Vilna. She was a successful merchant, just like her husband, and a strong-willed, firm mother. Her children and grandchildren, of whom Mama was the oldest, paid greater homage, gave more *koved* to her than anyone else in the family. They sought her advice, they telephoned her daily, they visited often.

One of the ways to pay homage to another person, I'd been taught by Mama, was to dress as carefully and nicely as means permitted when paying a visit, or receiving guests in one's home. Perhaps it was an edict that she'd learned from Bobbe Reise. Whatever the source, when Mama went to see her grandmother, in her large and beautiful apartment, she dressed as if she were visiting royalty. Mama would wear her most fashionable dress or nicest suit and always her newest, most becoming hat. When she came home, she sometimes told me that Bobbe Reise planned to buy an identical hat and that Mama was going with her to the milliner's shop the very next day. Even when I was very small, I'd wonder how my very young Mama and very old Great-grandmother could wear identical hats. Mama always seemed to take it as a great compliment.

One of Mama's regular duties for Bobbe Reise was to be present at sessions with the representative of one of Vilna's best jewelers. The man would come to the house to restring Bobbe Reise's huge strand of pearls. In those days, I think, there were no cultured pearls, only the real thing. Mama and Bobbe Reise sat near the jeweler at the dining-room table and made small talk while keeping a close watch over the pearls.

Mama told me about these visits and said that the pearls would one day be hers, and then mine, for she was the oldest granddaughter and I the oldest great-granddaughter. But she never took me along for the restringing ceremony, a sight I would have loved to have in my bank of memories.

Although Mama obviously loved her, Bobbe Reise could also make her angry. The anger was always brought on by Bobbe Reise's less than unconditional love for Mama's second mother and for Margola and Liusik. Where this antipathy began is buried in family lore, but I remember verbal battles Mama fought on behalf of her younger sister and brother and their mother. She was determined that Bobbe Reise's love, attention and help, when needed, was equal to that lavished on other grandchildren in the family. Mama's second mother, and the two younger children, were left in somewhat reduced circumstances after Grandfather died and all his great amounts of money, held in bank notes and paper currency, were calamitously devalued after World War I.

My own feelings for Bobbe Reise were not always clear and still aren't. I loved her and feared her. Her austere, imperious manner was sometimes unsettling. When I was little and went to visit her with my cousin Mussik, or with my parents, or Margola and Liusik, or all by myself, I came away not only with feelings of familial respect, but of fear that I'd been taught very important lessons which I'd better remember until the day I die. If I didn't, my place in Heaven would surely be taken by someone better, smarter and more deserving.

Bobbe Reise's lessons are well remembered, yet I am not always able to practice what she taught. One day, when I was seven or eight, I told her that on my way to school I often gave all or part of my sandwich to a beggar who sat on a nearby street corner. We sat alone at her dining-room table and she nodded with what I thought was approval. All at once she raised her strong hand and pointed a finger in my direction. "You are never to tell of your own good deeds. They will be immediately erased from the tablet on which God keeps count of our acts of charity. Charity given anonymously is the only charity that matters."

When I send contributions now to good causes and expect receipts or notes of thanks, or a listing in my synagogue bulletin, I worry about the propriety of such acknowledgment in the eyes of the Almighty, and equally so in the eyes of Bobbe Reise. I might meet her in the next world and her finger and gaze will be pointed in my direction. It is her eyes I fear most: hazel, narrow, all-knowing, piercing.

She expected much of her own children. Each of her daughters married happily to men with impeccable lineage. Rivka's learned, charitable husband was also as rich as Croesus, or so people said. To me he was kind Uncle Lippe, imposing but quiet. Rivka and Lippe had two daughters, one son and several grandchildren.

Their apartment was the biggest and most sumptuous I'd ever seen. My parents' wedding was held in its salon. When her children had the temerity to suggest that Bobbe Reise live with one of them, she marched through Rivka's huge house, my mother in tow (she'd told me the story years later) and demanded that her daughter tell her the purpose of each of her rooms.

"Well," Rivka said, "this is the salon, that is the dining room, and here is Lippe's study. Those are the children's rooms [though by then none lived at home] and in the back, of course, is the kitchen and the servants' quarters."

"Not one of them is called 'Mama's room,' is it?" Bobbe Reise quietly asked. "There are no Mama's rooms in children's houses." She would, therefore, continue to live independently, she said, with her devoted housekeeper for company during the day.

Her second daughter, Leah, married a quiet and scholarly man from Warsaw, where they lived in the 1930s. A daughter of theirs married a man who was one of the world's great experts on Esperanto, a language he hoped would be universally spoken and be a bond for people of all nations. Alas, this did not happen, nor do I ever hear talk of it now. When I was young it was often discussed at our dining-room table.

Bobbe Reise's youngest daughter, Yocha, married late. Her husband was a sweet shopkeeper in Vilna. It was this aunt of my mother's, and her two daughters, who survived the war and who told me about the fate of the rest of the family. They are more than Mama's cousins to me; they are two of my very best, most beloved friends.

Great-grandmother's sons prospered and were charitable men, just as she had taught them to be. Her oldest, Mama's father, was a lumber merchant until World War I. He died in his forties of heart failure like his own father.

Her second and favorite son, Yankl—Jacob in Hebrew—was also a lumber dealer in Vilna, well-to-do and well thought of. Late in life he married a young, bossy woman; they had two sons. His death and that of his older son brought about Bobbe Reise's decision to die.

Her third son, Max, went to America when he was quite young. He was unwilling to pursue any studies, nor help Bobbe Reise in business. With her approval and blessing, and money she'd provided, he left their home. After a difficult start, he made a success of his men's sportswear business and married a woman from Boston. She thought her lineage, or *yiches*, was better than that of the Cabots and Lodges, not to speak of the Cunzers of Vilna. Great-aunt Ida and Great-uncle Max (whose American surname was Hillson) were married for more than a half century and died when they were very old. They had no children.

It was for Great-uncle Max's synagogue that the Torah was written in Bobbe Reise's home in Vilna. Though I don't ever remember going to services with her, I recall seeing *yeshivah* students in her home—studying, praying, eating at her table. It was customary, almost incumbent upon those who could afford it, to take in impoverished students "*oif kest.*" This expression signaled that they were fed and clothed and lacked for nothing so that they could concentrate better on their studies of Torah and Gemara, Talmud and Mishnah, and other holy scriptures. A real *mitzvah*, a good deed for the entire family, and for Judaism, too.

Bobbe Reise was either asked by her son Max or she herself made the offer to engage a scribe to write the Torah for her son's congregation in New York. In the 1920s he became a staunch supporter of the late Rabbi Mordecai Kaplan, founder of Reconstructionist Judaism and of the Society for the Advancement of Judaism synagogue. Rabbi Kaplan, a charismatic leader and brilliant teacher, gathered about him not only scholars and students but people like Great-uncle Max, who gave him moral and financial backing.

Reconstructionist Judaism, preached at the Society for the Advancement of Judaism, emphasized the historical and rational aspects of our religion. Years before the practice became widely accepted, it welcomed the participation of women in all aspects of synagogue services. This appealed to my great-uncle and his wife. Its teachings, however, were far removed from Bobbe Reise's upbringing and the practices of her Orthodox ancestors.

Reconstructionists and the SAJ, as the Society is known, met with grave opposition from the Orthodox community in New York. While rabbis in America publicly denounced and even burned prayerbooks published by Rabbi Kaplan and his followers, a Torah was written for that congregation's ark in the home of a widow descended from a long line of Orthodox rabbis in Vilna.

Bobbe Reise herself would have been undaunted, I think, at the services conducted by Rabbi Kaplan. If she sat behind a *mechitze*, the curtain separating women from men in the small house of prayer in Lubtch, when she was a young girl and woman, or later in Vilna where it was not necessarily the norm, she had the mind of a progressive person. I can easily imagine her striding up the aisle, ascending the *bimah*, the pulpit, and accepting an *Aliyah* before the reading of a section in the Torah. She'd do it faultlessly, in a strong and echoing voice.

Her son Yankl carried the Torah in a special case to New York. He and his brother, Max, and sister-in-law presented it to Rabbi Kaplan sometime during the 1930s. A traditional weddinglike ceremony to install the Torah in the ark of the SAJ synagogue took place during a Sabbath morning service. A magnificent silver crown and breastplate were presented by Great-aunt Ida's relatives and placed on the Torah.

Years ago, in the 1940s and 1950s, when we met at Great-uncle Max's house, I found Rabbi Kaplan to be a remarkable human being. He was warm and caring, a man who asked wonderful questions. I remember those better than his lectures or comments. What's more, he loved Yiddish and spoke it with relish and elegance. But I could not, and still find it difficult, to attend services at the Society for the Advancement of Judaism.

I believe in miracles more than in historical facts and rational explanations, which Rabbi Kaplan and his many adherents consider the basis of our religion.

Miracles may seldom happen. But that my Bobbe Reise could ordain her own death without breaking Judaic law is a miracle. That the Torah written in her house over sixty years ago, in Vilna, is read and studied by many, that my family and I held it in our arms in the SAJ synagogue but two streets from my home in New York, is surely another.

Tata/Papa

Since the day I began to speak, quite early in life, I've called my father Tata, which in Polish means Daddy. Later, when I learned Yiddish, I sometimes pronounced it Tateh, but he was Tata most often throughout the years of my childhood and during our time in Siberia, even though in Russia everyone called their father Papa. When I finally began to call him Papa I cannot say, but it was not so very long ago.

He introduces himself as Tata to all of my old and new friends, for he is exceedingly proud of his "role" in my book about our lives in Siberia, where he is lovingly, admiringly and frequently referred to as Tata. He even signs copies of the book when I am not around, with his first and last name, and the words "Tata, the hero of this story."

At ninety years he is as naïve in some ways as he is

razor-sharp in others. His enthusiasm is boundless. A new flavor of ice cream is "wonderful, wonderful." Everything good is twice praised. Upon hearing a CD player for the first time in David's room he said to his grandson: "David, it doesn't pay to die; technology is so wonderful, wonderful!" Exactly those words, with a short pause where I put in the semicolon, and enormous excitement where the exclamation mark appears.

During one of my visits with Miss Rachel in Israel she told me that over the years she'd known many fathers and their children, but she had never observed a father who was "so at one" with his child. It was as if I were his very *neshomah*—soul in Yiddish, but with more meaning in that language than a translation provides. I felt it in my childhood and during the years we had together in Siberia—this constant outpouring of love and of pride. Telling him good news in person, or over the telephone, has been one of life's great pleasures for me. He oohs and aahs unreservedly and loudly, asks endless questions on the whys and wherefores of each situation, finds all the myriad reasons why this is wonderful, wonderful, and compliments not only the bearer of the good news, me, but also himself for having had a part in the bargain. For after all, he is my father! For him *naches* is a form of interest to be collected daily.

Rachel also told me that Tata said to her years ago in Vilna, when she first came to work with me at our house, that if God granted him one child only he wished that the child be a boy. I looked at her in panic, though I was fifty-seven years old when she told me what Papa had said to her when I was no more than five. To me he'd invariably said, with great emotion, "If God granted me one child only, I am so happy it is a daughter!" I told Rachel that *those* were his words ever since I could remember.

"You should have listened better to what I was saying," she laughed. "His statement was always made in the past tense!" Always a teacher, always ready to test me!

In 1939 Tata was drafted into the army as he had been when he was nineteen at the tail end of World War I. At age forty, he was sent to fight the Nazi invasion of Poland. The Polish army was overcome by the Nazis in a matter of weeks. Troops were disbanded, told to fend for themselves, throw away their dog tags, flee and save their lives. Tata found himself in a small forest, not knowing where he was or how to make his way to a place where someone might know him and give help. His dog tag was found, and in the confusion of those times, a notice arrived at our home that Papa had been killed.

Mama, with her unfailing ESP assured me and everyone, including the rabbi, that Papa would come back. Most of the family thought she'd lost her mind, and everyone treated her gingerly. One sister-in-law went so far as to say that since Tata was dead, and Mama too "distraught" to participate in the running of the store, perhaps our share of the store's income should be curtailed. Grandfather was so outraged that she was henceforth not welcome to visit him and Grandmother Anna in their home.

While all this commotion and furor was swirling in our usually peaceful enclave, Mama was her naturally stoic, controlled self, awaiting Papa's return in due course.

Margola was sent by Grandmother to live with us to

protect her dear sister, and me, from descent into total madness. Nothing could have been further from descent into madness than our house, but no one outside it would believe it.

Tata's situation, however, was desperate, though we did not learn about it until much later. The first night in the forest he took off his uniform and threw it away. He was left in long underwear and undershirt without his army boots, which would have revealed his army identity, his coat and hat. Curiously, he said, he kept his rifle. He made a place among twigs and leaves and lay quietly. German troops and tanks swirled all about. He told us that the chains of one tank were no more than two meters from where he hid on the ground. One more turn of the tank wheel and he'd have been as flat as the earth.

When morning came, the German army was gone, forging their way east. He, therefore, decided to proceed west, deeper into German-occupied Poland, but away from the battlefields and our home in Vilna. He walked along a road on which many refugees sought escape from the occupying forces, but who barely preceded the Germans in their sorry flight. Along the way these refugees dropped their clothes, bedding and other goods to lighten the bags they carried. He picked up a beret, a blanket and a safety pin, put the first on his head, arranged the second around his shoulders, and fastened the blanket with the pin. If anyone stopped him, he would pretend that he was a madman. He probably looked the part.

He had some money in a leather porte-monnaie, a small change purse used by gentlemen in Europe. This he put in his underwear or carried in his fist. He walked all day on the side of the road, hidden from main highways. Toward nightfall he stopped at a farm and asked to stay the night. The Polish farm couple was reluctant to permit it, not because he was a Jew—they hardly could suspect it—but because they feared he was either mad or a deserter. He hid his rifle under the blanket, but perhaps they observed it.

After earnest pleas and an offer of money, the couple told him he could go into the barn. Later they sent over a child with bread and a mug of milk. When Tata tells this story it always stays the same, told in nearly identical words, as if on a recording or in a film. It is etched on his brain more than any part of his long life. He repeatedly bemoans the fact that because he'd lost much weight, he lost his wedding ring with which he married Mama, in the haystack of that barn. It pleases me to hear that the ring meant so much to him then, and still does, in every retelling. I loved seeing my parents in identical plain gold bands; he never replaced the one that was lost.

After spending the night in the barn he continued to walk stealthily, still barefoot, with the soles of his feet covered with sores and caked blood, until he reached a small village one afternoon. A small pawn shop, of all things, was open. It stocked old clothes, shoes and hats. Tata went in, and with the bit of money still left in his porte-monnaie, and by pawning his rifle, he got socks, a pair of ragged old pants that barely reached his ankles, an old shirt and a greasy jacket, as well as a pair of shoes, which turned out to be too tight and which he carried on his back instead of wearing on his feet.

He asked around for a post office. One was nearby. He

wanted to send a letter to us to reassure us that he was alive. He found his way to the building, but when he got there, he realized that he'd forgotten his change purse and the bit of money in it in the pawn shop. When he ran back the porte-monnaie was gone. The shopkeeper gave him money to buy a stamp, but the post office was closed by the time he returned there.

Papa dared not linger in that little town for fear his presence would be noticed and the S.S. police would become suspicious. The pawnbroker explained how he could get to Czestochowa, the nearest large city. Papa had business associates in Czestochowa whose names and addresses he remembered. Fifty years later he still does, with perfect clarity.

After walking some two hundred or more kilometers, he arrived in Czestochowa, dirty, unshaven, looking like a beggar. He forced his bloody, swollen feet into the too small shoes and walked to the home of very good customers of his, who were also friends, and also Jewish.

At first they did not recognize him and were reluctant to let him in. But when he reminded them of details in their business dealings that only he could have known and named the people they'd had to dinner the last time he was in their city, they were convinced—and appalled at his condition. He remembers the hot bath in their home as one of the most luxuriant moments of his life. These good people let him stay in a small servant's room behind the kitchen, with the understanding that he'd be quiet and make himself as invisible as possible.

The reign of terror by the Nazis had begun, but in

September of 1939 the Czestochowa ghetto had not yet been formed. S.S. troops made forays into homes, schools, businesses; every suspicious, unaccounted for, undocumented person was shot on sight. The family that took Tata in shared with him their small food rations, shielded him and spoke with him in tightly guarded secrecy.

The son of the family, whom Tata calls "an aristocrat" in bearing and nature, was kinder to him than a brother. He would have done anything for Tata, but all my father wanted was to let us know he was alive. To send letters to Vilna from Czestochowa or to telephone was simply not possible; that is what bothered Tata most. He speaks of the family as *tzaddikim,* the holiest of men and women in Jewish tradition.

When it became known that Hitler and Stalin made a peace pact, and that people could apply for exit visas from German-occupied Poland to Soviet-occupied territories, Tata took courage in hand and went to the German city prefecture to apply for traveling papers. He claimed that all his documents had been lost in a fire, gave his first name not as Samuel but Stanislaw (his last name sounded Polish already). His appearance was Aryan; it helped.

Miraculously a visa was granted, and he began to arrange the journey back to Vilna. A railroad ticket, however, was expensive. Much clandestine planning was necessary to make passage possible, including a loan, which he received on faith and which he promised to repay to the lender's family once he got to Warsaw, where he had to stop on his way to Vilna. Mama's aunt Leah, Bobbe Reise's daughter and sister of Mama's late father, lived in Warsaw; she would lend him money to repay the people from Czestochowa. Papa recalls that generosity and faith in the honesty of others existed even under the most difficult conditions.

Papa's friends in Czestochowa outfitted him in dapper clothes, which had belonged to another friend who sought refuge with them but was arrested and sent to a concentration camp or executed in a street "action." Before Papa left them he promised that they would all celebrate together when the war was over. No one really knew, even then, in western Poland, how the war would end for the Jews.

Tata received a letter from his benefactors after his return to Vilna. Much of it was written by the son Papa had called an aristocrat, and with whom he'd developed such a friendship. A postscript by the young man's father, Papa's business associate, said that the son had been caught by the S.S. that very day on the street and shot without reason. People they knew saw it and reported the tragic news. The father decided to send the letter anyway, for it was meant for Tata. And miraculously it reached him; it came as if from the next world. After Tata had read it, he hit his desk in despair and cried inconsolably for hours. That, of course, happened after the miracle of his reappearance at home in Vilna, and runs far ahead of this recounting of Tata's own long and arduous journey.

The letter Tata sent us just before leaving Czestochowa did not reach us—ever. Many, most letters in those days never reached their destinations. We knew nothing of his stay in Czestochowa, nor that he was on his way back to Vilna.

When Tata arrived in Warsaw, he immediately went to

Great-aunt Leah's house. What he found in the Jewish quarter of Warsaw appalled him. It was already a clear precursor of what the Warsaw ghetto, all ghettos, would be like. Jews were crammed in together. Aunt Leah's once spacious apartment was like the proverbial sardine can. Papa borrowed money from someone who wanted to send cash to Vilna, squared his account with his Czestochowa loan "bank." He did not have enough money for a train ticket to Vilna from Warsaw, but he'd heard of several actors from the world-famous Vilna Yiddish Theater Troupe who were stranded in Warsaw by the war. Led by an actor with one wooden leg, they were hiring a wagon to take them to Bialystok, not far from Vilna. Why they went to Bialystok and not to Vilna Papa can no longer recall. He participated in the expenses of hiring horse and wagon, and thought he'd have enough cash to buy a railroad ticket to Vilna from Bialystok.

All these events took place in a period of six or seven weeks in the fall of 1939, but it seemed an eternity to me then. During the week that Papa was on his way back to Vilna by train, wagon and train again, Mama was galvanized into action. On October 12 she announced that Papa would return home within a week. By then Margola, Liusik, Grandmother, all the aunts and uncles and grandparents in our compound decided that she had definitely lost her mind. She was in a frenzy of preparation for Tata's return; she cleaned the house, whacked the carpets with straw wickets, scrubbed windows, washed clothes. Our housekeeper, Yulia, had left for her village home when the first bombs fell in early September, but Mama did not need household assistance when she chose to do without it. She was a fanatical, systematic house cleaner then, and until the end of her life. She's probably making certain there's no dust in Heaven, either, wearing old white gloves as she did at home, checking to see that all surfaces are spotless. Even the tops of doors guarded by Father Abraham or our matriarchs may fall under her scrutiny.

After our home in Vilna was clean enough to meet even her high standards, she stormed throughout the city, searching for just the right kind of farmer cheese, not too soft and not too dry, just the way Tata liked it, for tinned pineapple slices, which he enjoyed and which seemed the height of luxury in my childhood, and strawberry preserves.

On the evening of October 15 all was ready. I went to bed early since school had once again begun and Margola was back in university classes. Mama had a headache and went to sleep also.

In the morning Margola walked with me to school and continued on to the university campus not too far from our home. At about the same time Tata was disembarking from the train from Bialystok at the Vilna train station. He stopped at the home of Mama's mother, hoping that together she, Margola and Liusik would prepare my mother for the amazing event that was to happen—his rising up from the dead.

When Grandmother opened the door in answer to his knock, she threw both hands to her mouth and cried out: "Mulinka, you *are* here! And I did not make your favorite chicken!" Tata does not exaggerate events and words. If anything, he plays down stories. I, therefore, know that

Grandmother's first words to Tata as he appeared at her door "resurrected" must have been precisely those he remembers and repeats with love and a sad, sweet smile. Perhaps if she had trusted Mama's intuition she would have prepared the pullet with browned potatoes and a carrot *tzimmes*, which Tata said no one made as wonderfully as she!

Grandmother and Liusik escorted Tata to our house, where Mama was, of course, thrilled but not at all surprised to see him. And she did have his favorite cheese, so her words of welcome likely differed from her own mother's.

Margola was called at the university and came to get me at my own school. I remember how she and the principal tried to prepare me, gently, for the shock. I cannot imagine why, because I was not shocked; I was ecstatic. We ran all the way home, Margola and I, and I remember repeating over and over like a song refrain, "Mama told me, Mama told me, Mama told me!"

When the door opened, I hurled myself at Tata. I don't remember what was said or done on October 16, 1939, but two days later was my parents' anniversary and my cousin Salik's and my birthdays, and the celebration that year lasted for days. Some of the festivities were held in Grandfather and Grandmother's home across the stairwell from ours. All the rooms, including Aunt Sonitchka's, were filled with relatives, friends and business associates.

Not long after Tata's return in October, Vilna was returned to Lithuania by the Soviets and became Vilnius, the capital, as it has been off and on for centuries. Lithuanian was taught in all schools, including in my Yiddish Folk Shul where it replaced Polish in the curriculum. All that I remember of Lithuanian is the words for "I do not understand Lithuanian."

Times for Vilna residents, including Jews, seemed stable, with good business and plentiful food. But the lovely hiatus of peace and prosperity in our lives was shattered when the three Baltic countries, Estonia, Latvia and Lithuania, were annexed by the Soviet Union. The newspapers and radio broadcasts to which we listened on our beautiful new Telefunken radio, with nearly as many keys as a small accordion, proclaimed that the three countries wanted to join the great USSR, a "joke" discussed secretly in homes and coffee houses. This "joining" of countries was traumatic for us.

In June of 1941, at six in the morning, Russian soldiers stormed into Grandfather and Grandmother's house. My uncle Dodzia saw the trucks parked in front of the entrance and telephoned Papa that something was terribly wrong. He asked Papa to go across the stairwell landing to investigate what was happening in their parents' apartment; his was at the other end of the building, reached by a different door or through our communal garden.

Such are fate's vagaries. Had Uncle Dodzia gone to see what was happening at his parents' home, not Papa, perhaps it would have been he, his wife Musia and their beautiful, energetic son whose lives would have been saved by deportation to Siberia, not Tata's, Mama's and mine.

Tata, still in his pajamas, was made to sit on the floor of his parents' apartment, along with his dignified seventy-two-year-old father, and tiny, elegant, furious Grandmother

Anna. While Tata was gone, Mama sent me to the home of her mother, Margola and Liusik, with all her best jewelry stuck into a large kitchen matchbox. I ran like a mouse pursued by a cat, gave the box to Grandmother, kissed her, Margola and Liusik, and ran back to Mama without knowing or being able to tell them what was really happening in our "peaceful" family compound.

Just as Tata was being led into our apartment by soldiers with bayonets, I ran into the apartment through the back door, which led into our garden. We were all made to sit on the floor of our dining room and charged with the crime of being capitalists and enemies of the people and, therefore, to be deported to the depths of the Soviet Union. When we were being loaded onto the trucks by the soldiers, like so many sacks of potatoes, my cousin Sanna came running toward us, sobbing inconsolably. She threw to me the tiny, simple medallion she always wore, where the Ten Commandments were written on the enamel. I had it hidden in Siberia, and now it lies in our bank safe for fear I'll lose it. I know it is in the dark confines of the vault, but I go there periodically to check just the same.

We spent nearly six years on the steppe, three of those without Papa. He was drafted into the army one more time, at age forty-four, and went through basic training in Siberia. While in Novosibirsk, Papa went to the circus on his day off. Only he would choose such entertainment. While at the performance, he discovered a very distant relative of his who'd run away from home as a young boy and who was walking the high wire as an acrobat with the troupe.

Papa walked a high wire of his own during his years

fighting the German armies on the Russian front. He had many harrowing experiences along the way, to be sure, but the one he repeats to this day is relatively minor. He left his spoon in one of the trenches, and he said over and over, "An old soldier is totally lost without his spoon." He had no way of eating his ration of soup with bits of potatoes, vegetables and sometimes even meat. Since soldiers got good rations of vodka to help them erase from their minds the reality of battle, he traded his ration with a young boy for that soldier's spoon. The boy did not mind slurping his soup like a puppy.

I am sure that when Tata shot from the trenches, he prayed that he killed the enemy without killing people. It is nearly impossible to imagine Tata, who could not kill a mouse, dealing with war's ravages on a man-to-man level. Yet his battalion reached the river Elbe, where they met American and British troops in the closing months of World War II; the battles they fought on the way to Berlin were many and fierce.

He seldom speaks of those days now; it is the experiences in 1939 that he most often recalls. But Papa, even at ninety, does not live in the past. Every day, every month, every year holds fresh hope for him. He is determined to live his day-to-day life to the fullest.

Nearly two years after Mama died, he married again at seventy-two. His second wife, Mrs. E., and her first husband knew Papa and Mama when they were all young in Vilna, and later on in New York. During the Nazi terror in Vilna, she, her two young boys and her husband hid in a primitive cellar—really a hole under a barn floor—on the farm of a

Polish family they'd known in the 1930s. Mrs. E. and her family could not stand up during the time they were hidden. All their days and nights were spent in a sitting position, and all their bodily needs were met under the most cramped, inhuman conditions. But all four survived.

Papa's second wife was not well during most of the twelve years of their marriage, and he nursed her and took care of her in an uncommonly gallant, loving manner.

When the couple who saved Papa's second wife and her family, and whom her sons still support in a generous and solicitous way, came to visit New York from Poland, something quite extraordinary happened. The Gentile couple remembered Papa from Vilna; the man had bought from him the most modern, expensive tools and parts for repairing his cars and farm machinery in the mid-1930s. "The tools still work beautifully," the man told Papa. "You always urged me to get the best money could buy so they'd last me a lifetime! You were right, they did!"

Papa repeats with zest this exchange of remembrances with his second wife's savior. As they talked of their long lives, the war and its aftermath, the man told him that most of his friends in Lodz or in Warsaw still don't know that he'd saved four Jews. He is afraid of their reaction to him, a Jew-loving Pole. This was one of the few times in the past decade that I saw a look of absolute despair on the face of my father. Will "IT" (anti-Semitism is often referred to as "IT" in my family) never cease, he asked me?

But with Papa despair passes quickly. Every morning is full of promise. He wants to know everything that happens in our lives. As soon as I call him between eight and nine, his first question is, "And what did you accomplish today?"

"I got up!" I reply, and we both laugh, he much more brightly than I. When he asks the same question in the evening, as he is used to getting a call from me then, too, laughter comes less easily to me. Some days I've accomplished little, can report nothing that would make him bubble, nor give him the *naches* he expects from me daily. On such evenings I think of my daughter's apt description of what parents expect their children to be—"*naches* machines"—performing faultlessly on an infinite schedule.

Papa himself almost always has something wonderful, wonderful to report on his day. The Lincoln Center Library had just the movie cassette he wanted to borrow. He saw the most incredible science program on channel 13. The *Jerusalem Post* or the *Jewish Week* had the most brilliant essay on Israeli politics or culture.

At all times he is an incurable optimist, but calls himself a *fantaseur*, a word he claims is Russian, sounds French when he says it, and I think he simply invented to suit his own needs and temperament. This particular *fantaseur*, or fantasy-follower-seeker-fancier, claims that without an element of fantasy none of the great inventions of mankind would have been born. Years and years after hearing this theory, I found an article in *The New York Times* that espoused the same notion in a literate and scientific manner. I sent it to my father in Miami Beach. He was delighted and let no time pass before he called me with a victorious, "Aha, you see, the *Times* agrees with me!" As far as I know, he'd decided that the *Times* reporter got the idea from him by osmosis.

Unlike the *Times* reporter, Papa cites examples, chapter

and verse, from Jules Verne's novels, which he firmly says became truth in the twentieth century. As for Albert Einstein's theory of relativity, only a *fantaseur* would have come up with that one. All of them, he claims, have common denominators: flights of fancy, imagination, daring to dream and plan the impossible.

Papa would likely be happiest if he discovered that Jules Verne was Jewish or that the Wright brothers spoke Yiddish at home. He needn't worry about Albert Einstein, and Isaac Newton sounds quite Jewish to him. And how about Samuel Morse? Samuel was one of our great prophets, and it is a Jewish name. And could "Morse" have been something else when his ancestors came to America? I've learned not to argue.

No matter whom I meet, hear about, read of or mention, his first question is invariably, "Is he, or she, or even it, Jewish?" My son, David, once asked whether Grandpa is bigoted. I assured him that Grandpa is not. It simply pleases him to hear, or to think that a lot of people in the world, especially those we love and admire or who have done something special, are Jewish. At the same time, learning of crooks, gangsters and other shady characters who are Jewish makes him nearly hysterical. "They pollute our garden!" he shouts at no one in particular, but most often at the TV screen or at the daily newspaper in his lap.

He has intense feelings on the subject of converts to Judaism. I first learned how deeply he felt when he met Rachel C., a friend of ours and a worshiper at Temple Ansohe Chesed to which he once also belonged. He was eighty-six years old then.

"Oh, what a lovely woman! What a wonderful, wonderful smile! Is she Jewish?" Since he had just met her at our synagogue, one would have assumed that the question would not have come up. Not so with my father.

When I told him she was a convert, he stopped in his tracks in the middle of crossing 96th Street and West End Avenue, pointed his finger at me, and sternly said, "Remember, you must honor her more than your father and mother! It says so in the book!" After I led him to the sidewalk, I asked which book had this marvelous injunction, not that I needed one to honor Rachel. "In Rashi's book," he said, and for him that settled the matter for all time. He was right, too. Rashi, the most venerated of Jewish theologians and commentators on the Torah, uses the words Tata quoted. Precisely.

As I. L. Peretz wrote in a wonderful story, though the context was different, "All Jews should do so well."

Raya

There are two little girls, one in Bethesda, Maryland, the other in Pawtucket, Rhode Island, who were named for Raya. The blond, brown-eyed beauty in Bethesda, with a merry smile and reserved manner, is called Rachel. Her mother thought it was Raya's Hebrew name. It wasn't, but the intention and love are all that matter. The baby in Pawtucket is named simply Raya. She has blue-gray eyes with long black lashes and a serenity that is astonishing.

Rachel's mother and Raya's father are twins. They are the children of one of Raya's cousins. Both told me why they named their younger children for Raya, to their mother's astonished pleasure. Each said that Raya was a vital part of their childhood. They recall her as outgoing and warm, loving, smiling and bearing armloads of gifts when she came to visit. A demonstrative, giving, hugging aunt named Raya. They were eighteen years old when she died.

Raya was my mother. In my own childhood she was not demonstrative—she seldom kissed or hugged me and that sometimes made me sad. When she did, the warmth and protectiveness of her arms around me, or a kiss on top of my hair, lasted in me a long, long time. I always felt greatly loved, just not kissed or hugged a lot by Mama.

Mama was not given to profligate compliments either. She nurtured me in a way that's easy to appreciate in looking back as an adult. Perhaps for a child it was too spare, too pointed. When she'd overhear me talking to myself, a habit I still have, she'd comment briefly: "You're speaking to a very smart person." Sometimes she'd pat my head and say, "You're in very good company." These dry words stay in my mind, they prop up my self-confidence when I need it now. She had a look of approbation, a slight nod of her head, when I shared news of something I'd accomplished, which was never effusive, yet meaningful when I was a child. The memory still is.

Later in life I found it difficult to share good news with her over the phone. I needed to see that nod and look in her eyes, for her voice was always even, never raised in disapproval as it was not in praise.

Her quiet love and confidence in me served me well during our years in Siberia. Someone jokingly said to Mama, and she repeated it to me without comment, that I walked around Rubtsovsk as if I were the daughter of the commissar. I did walk around "chin up," even when I had no shoes and wore patched old clothes. Her nod of approval followed the joke in a way I still remember. "Hold your head high always," it implied, as she herself did all of her life.

Mama was tall and imposing. She had a strongly arched Roman nose and green-gray-brown eyes that changed color with the clothes she wore. I never saw their like in others. She had a brilliant smile, and though I don't think she was vain, her perfectly white, beautiful teeth were undoubtedly a source of pride. When she lost them at age forty-four in New York to chronic gum disease acquired in Siberia, she must have been devastated. She never said so, but her smile was never the same.

Her skin was light and translucent, aided and abetted by a glass of hot water with juice of one lemon she drank every morning in Vilna. I found the custom peculiar. Her shiny, long, dark hair was braided and arranged in different patterns in back of her head. A manicurist came to our house at least once a week. Mama's hands were always perfectly groomed, although she was a craftswoman and worked with various materials, including clay. Her embroideries, ceramics and weavings were displayed and used by everyone in the family.

She dressed understatedly and elegantly before the war when she could afford it, and after the war when our means were more limited. When she bought a good dress or suit she'd say, "We're too poor to buy shoddy things." Excellence in all things was important to her.

Mama was a creative cook in her youth, though everyday meals were often prepared by our maid. She was the family's best baker—her napoleons, twelve-layer cakes, gossamer cookies and small Danish-like pastries melted in one's mouth. Mama's cousins recall that when the Feast of Purim came around, Bobbe Reise, as always, engaged a *yeshivah* student to come to her home and read the Megilla, which tells how Queen Esther thwarted Haman's evil plan to kill the Jews of Persia. "When Raya comes," Bobbe Reise would tell them, "we'll have a *true* feast." She'd arrive, the cousins still marvel, with the most incredible, enormous chocolate log and armloads of cookies and cakes and candied fruit. There are none like them in the best *patisserie* in Paris or even in a four-star restaurant in New York.

Perhaps her life during World War I had something to do with her love of baking. She told me that her family had to escape Vilna and live in Minsk for a time. While there, her father was in charge of a bakery, which assured them a steady supply of bread. Perhaps she longed for sweets as I did in wartime? Perhaps that bakery in Minsk did not produce anything but black, heavy bread?

Mama went to a convent school during the time the family spent in Minsk. For an observant Jew from Vilna to send his oldest child to a Catholic school, even briefly, was brave and adventurous for that time and place. Grandfather believed, Mama told me, that education was vital, whatever its source. Their faith and way of life was in no way threatened by nuns. Ever since then, Mama could recite the Rosary in perfect Latin, to the astonishment of our Catholic friends in this country.

After World War I the family returned to Vilna, and Grandfather had to start his lumber business from scratch. Whatever he'd saved was in worthless paper money. Many rooms in those days could have been wallpapered with such "savings." Mama said that he would have done well in his second start, but Grandfather had had a weak heart and died at age forty-nine.

Soon after his death her brother, Benjamin, who later brought us all to America, went to New York. He lived with his father's brother Max, worked in Max's business, endured Aunt Ida's high-handed ways, married Aunt Dorothy, who loved baseball, and had two children. Mama missed her brother Nioma, as was his Polish nickname, and kept pictures of him and his family throughout our home in Vilna. He was an important member of our clan, though I did not meet him until I arrived in New York in 1947.

At twenty-four, "old" for her time and place, I was later told, she married my father, whose family background in the merchant class in Vilna did not overwhelm Bobbe Reise with enthusiasm, a matter of amusement and glee in the family. His *yiches* or pedigree was some notches below Mama's family, and at the beginning of their marriage Bobbe Reise made sure he was properly aware of the wonderful match he'd made. When I was born, her first great-grandchild, all was well and forgiven.

Mama had had a number of miscarriages before I was born, and afterward, too. She never told me, of course; it would have been unseemly for her to discuss it with me. I heard of it years later, long after she died. Perhaps this was why she forbade me "dangerous" physical activities, not to speak of joy rides with Uncle Sioma. It must also have been the reason for many hated glasses of carrot juice and "gogl mogls," warm concoctions of milk, egg yolks and honey with which she tried to ward off disaster for me—and did.

During the Second World War, Mama's life was fraught with hardships, but she never made them an issue. She did not feel sorry for herself in 1939, in Vilna, when Papa was drafted into the Polish army and declared dead several weeks later. She didn't feel sorry for herself in Siberia, either. She made no complaint, though her existence was beset by illness, hunger, hard labor in a gypsum mine, festering sores on her legs and feet and excruciating attacks of sciatica. When Papa was drafted again in 1942, she provided not only physical but moral support for me, for Grandmother Anna but for friends in the community of deportees in Rubtsovsk. She was the rock against whom many rested. Mama overcame much without fuss or lament, a trait that she tried to pass on to me. Her success in that respect is only sporadic.

Her strong opinions on Yiddishkeit, on feminism, though not called by that name, on being a *mensch* and helping others were carefully planted and watered, too. She showed by example, not only by word, that to give money, but not of oneself, wasn't enough.

Cooking a meal, scrubbing a floor, washing laundry— and bringing flowers—for someone who is ill, that was giving. She had a huge collection of plastic containers and foil plates that she lined up regularly on her kitchen table and filled with good things for friends who were ill, not able to cook or simply in need of a visit. Mama never arrived in anyone's house without shopping bags filled with delicious, carefully wrapped gifts. In my childhood her mother arrived similarly loaded. Grandmother never could ring our doorbell; her hands were always full. She stood with her back to the door and knocked with her shoe heel. I sometimes think I hear the same sound, and I remember the joy of letting her in. Mama and Grandmother never expected *koved*, honor or thanks. Their greatest pleasure was giving. A lesson easier to teach than to learn.

Mama instilled in me a love of Yiddish when she read me stories in that rich language and later when she enrolled me in the unpretentious Folk Shul in Vilna. Every subject in Sofia Markovna Gurewicz Elementary School was taught in Yiddish, and many of its children came from homes with means smaller than ours. That sometimes made me feel guilty for having more than some of my school friends. All of my cousins attended a well-known Jewish private school, Epstein's Gymnasium, where Polish was the official language and so-called middle- and upper-class children were in the vast majority.

As soon as I was old enough to have my own library card, Mama registered me in the CBK Library, Vilna's famous "Centrale Bibliotek far Kinder," and put me under the unfaltering eye and care of its children's librarian, Dina Abramowicz. (She is now the librarian emeritus at the YIVO Institute in New York, and when she nods with approval at something I've done, it makes me feel very accomplished.) Mama and Dina made sure that I read not only Polish translations of *Anne of Green Gables*, and writers like Mark Twain, Hugh Lofting, Frances Hodgson Burnett and endless mysteries, but works of classical and modern writers and poets in Yiddish, as well.

Yet Mama was hardly provincial or fanatic in her devotion to all things Yiddish and Jewish. She was, throughout her life, and under all circumstances, open-minded and outspoken.

She did not hesitate to set me straight when she thought

my words or behavior were wrong or obtuse. One day, in my first semester at Hunter College, a nice girl came up to speak to me in the cafeteria. I had very few American friends; most of my high-school classmates went to out-of-town universities. Walter, who was my best friend in every respect, was on tour most of that year. I felt quite alone, and too shy to begin conversations.

When I came home I told Mama all about Lily. "She's so wonderful, so smart and so friendly." I listed Lily's other, numerous virtues. I ended by saying, "But she's not Jewish." Mama sat still at the table in our small apartment in Brooklyn. "How would you feel if Lily told her mother how wonderful you are but that you're Jewish?" She looked as stern as Bobbe Reise did when she pointed out one of my failings in Vilna.

Mama seldom gave advice and she never lectured. A question, a comment, a word here or there, were full of life-shaping ideas. Before Walter and I married, she suggested that we must have a serious talk. That alarmed me, for we'd never before had a *serious talk*. The thought of my private and reserved mother discussing a *serious* matter filled me with panic.

She wanted to tell me, I learned later, that I should always have my own money. "Start with five dollars, but keep your own bank account, to do with as you like, to answer to no one." These were startling words, for in childhood I never got an allowance. However, my relief that this was the subject of our *serious talk* was as great as the wisdom of her advice.

Now that I have children of marriageable age, I am surprised that Mama never questioned my plans to get married at age nineteen, to a man nine years older than I, of a different cultural background, with very special interests, and the difficult schedule of a concert pianist, which we would have to follow in our life together. And a man who did not consider Yiddish a proper language but a form of Mittel-Hoch-Deutsch! This had indeed caused anxious moments at the dinner table when Walter first came to visit, with loud protests and heated outbursts on my part, and quiet, scholarly and expert assertions from Mama. Hers, if not mine, of course prevailed, and the time arrived when Walter became convinced of the importance of Yiddish. He now refers to it as "Mame Loshen," or our "Mother Tongue," and tries to speak it as enthusiastically as do those of us from Vilna.

Mama's love and interest in Vilna never waned, and she worked very hard for a cultural organization, in New York, called *Nusach Vilna*; the essence, the meaning of Vilna is what *nusach* means. This group of men and women have sponsored, and still do, lectures on Yiddish literature, books of special meaning, gatherings at which Yiddish poets and writers share their work. She spent countless hours addressing letters exhorting people to attend, to read new Yiddish books, to remember Vilna.

At the same time, she was vehement that we should never go back to visit. This opposition, so out of keeping with her usual live-and-let-live outlook, never abated. To Mama, Vilna was VILNA when it was the seat of Jewish culture, not Vilnius, the capital of Lithuania, where on Ponar there isn't a mention that thousands of Jews died there at the hands of the Nazis.

"Don't make a ruin of your wonderful memories!" For

years I thought that I would not listen to her exhortation, that I would go. But now I am not so sure. Perhaps she was right. Perhaps memories should not be tampered with.

When Mama was stricken with incurable cancer, she was sixty-six years old. Her health was frail during the years she lived in America, but to me she was invincible. She survived so much, so bravely and resolutely; she would beat this, too. She took on cancer as she did everything else in her life, with utter self-control, without self-pity, save for one outburst in her three-month-long stay in a New York hospital.

During a painful test, the specialist who administered it complimented her on her stoicism during the difficult procedure. She was the most cooperative patient he'd ever had. She cried out, "Give me no compliments, doctor! I want to live! Help me live!" The doctor, the interns, the nurse and I were silent. I left quickly and hid in the washroom—and sobbed. For I doubted by then that the doctors could help Mama.

I stayed with her from early morning until late at night in the hospital, neglecting my family, doing no work. Though Mama doted on her two grandchildren and showed her love with constant applause, hugs, kisses and presents, she could not bear to let me go home. "Stay just ten more minutes, Essinka, just ten minutes." It did not matter that the children were lonely, that Walter was away. Mama asked *me* to say, and I was there when she needed me.

It was the only time in our lives when she praised me each day. Everything I did for her was without equal. She used the most glistening Yiddish expressions when I changed her gown, rubbed her back, brushed her hair, wiped her face or fed her. She even found the perfect sound to let me know that no nurse could give her a bedpan as skillfully as I managed. A lifetime of unsaid compliments poured out; she needed to give them and I needed to hear them.

The night before she died she seemed to be in a coma. I stood by her bed in darkness except for the light in the corridor. As I stroked her arm, she suddenly spoke in strong, clear Yiddish. "Give me a kiss!" She said it again and again. "I will need your kisses where I am going." She who kissed me so seldom craved kisses desperately herself.

Her funeral, held in the largest chapel of the biggest funeral parlor in New York, was packed. No seat remained empty. The rabbi who officiated, but who barely knew her as he came to our synagogue during her illness, was amazed at the size of the gathering. After all, Mama was not a leader in the business community, nor a rich benefactress, but she was a *mensch* and everyone knew it.

The last eulogy was given by Lazar E., a remarkable old social activist from Vilna, who for a time lived in China and worked with Mao Tse-tung. His only son and John Hersey were best friends, when both were young, in that far-off land. Lazar spoke in classical Yiddish, the language Mama loved best of all. Though many of our friends did not understand its literal meaning, they understood and still recall its sound and emotion.

"Now Raya, too, is gone," the small, hunchbacked, unforgettable man said, as if her death followed those of other great figures in Jewish history. "We shall miss her presence." Lazar spoke simply and quietly of her humanity, her

219

devotion to Yiddishkeit, the perpetuation of our language, our culture, our heritage, our people.

Lazar's words evoked a scene from my childhood. I remembered sitting with Mama at our dining-room table where she taught me to write the Yiddish alphabet, the Aleph-Bet-Gimmel-Dalet. Mama put before me a small, lined notebook with a brown cover. I bought a nearly identical notebook in Jerusalem when I began writing this book. Next to my notebook Mama placed a well-sharpened pencil and a brand-new eraser.

She watched my hand and insisted that I copy every letter carefully and firmly. Then she made me erase each one. I had to repeat this on many lines, writing the entire Yiddish alphabet, then erasing each letter under her watchful gaze. Over and over I had to do it until the entire page was filled. When I stopped, Mama made me look carefully in the places where I had written the letter *yud*.

This *yud* looks like an exclamation point with the period under it. In Yiddish it is the middle of three letters that spell *Jew*; in Hebrew it's the first letter in the word *Israel*. While all the letters of the alphabet were erasable, the period in *yud* was still clearly visible on my notebook page.

She pointed to it. "Remember, my child, the *pintelle yid*, the dot that is part of the word that says who we are, cannot be erased. It will always be here if we write it firmly and strongly."

I try to do it strongly and firmly, not only when writing in Yiddish, but also when reflecting on what it means to be Jewish.